PLAIN TALK ABOUT COLLEGE

PLAIN TALK

ALSO BY ALLEN LUDDEN

PLAIN TALK FOR MEN UNDER 21!
PLAIN TALK FOR WOMEN UNDER 21!
ROGER THOMAS, ACTOR!

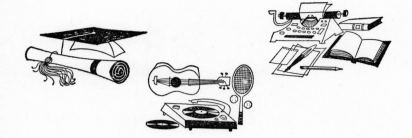

ABOUT COLLEGE

by ALLEN LUDDEN

Drawings by Rupert Finegold

DODD, MEAD & COMPANY : NEW YORK

1961

U. S. 1150013

FOR:

David, College Class of '70
Martha, College Class of '71
Sarah, College Class of '74

May I express my gratitude to . . .

MR. FRANK A. LOGAN, Assistant Director of Admissions at Dartmouth College, for his thoughtful comments . . .

MR. FRANK J. ADAMS, Director of Guidance for the Hastings-on-Hudson High School, for his careful guidance and instruction . . .

MR. W. H. SAHLOFF, Vice President of the General Electric Company, and to his associates for their support and belief in the "General Electric College Bowl" . . .

DR. HARRY RANSOM, President of the University of Texas, for his faith and encouragement . . .

MISS GRACE LOWN, typist extraordinary, for her ability to type and to correct my spelling.

And . . .

MARYE D. BENJAMIN, without whose talent and industry this book would never have been completed.

Sincerely,
Allen Ludden

CONTENTS

CONTENTS

PLAIN TALK ABOUT COLLEGE

A WORD BEFORE

COMPETITION is a way of life in America.

Up until graduation from high school, the competition a young person meets is, for the most part, a kind of child's play. The moment that high school diploma is put into the graduate's hand, however, the competition in his life becomes quite another thing. Suddenly, he faces a down-to-earth, coldly competitive race for success. From that point forward, the contest is for real. The BIG RACE is on! And the stakes are BIG, too: *Security* (in mind and body) and *Satisfaction.*

It's a rigorous contest that never lets up. From the moment the high school doors close behind the young American graduate, it *never lets up.*

Tough as it is, though, it's the best way. It's stimulating, challenging, and . . . it's *democratic:* each individual is free to do what he *can* do. It's up to him. How much he accomplishes, how much he wins, depends entirely upon his ability to compete with other free Americans.

Even when the race seems to be turning against him, no real American would want it any other way. No one who has tasted the precious dignity of freedom wants to lose it. Earnest, healthy, unrelenting competition between individuals is the *muscle* of freedom. So long as we live in a free, democratic society, we must have free, democratic competition between the individuals in that society.

Whenever the individual is protected, sheltered from the losses *and the wins* of individual competition, he moves away from a free way of life and toward a controlled society in which he, as an individual, means nothing and the group . . . or *state* . . . is the all-important concern.

Being so much a part of the American way of doing things, the competitive spirit is inherent in the personality of every young American long before he becomes a high school graduate. Ever since kindergarten he has been playing games to win. All through his school career he has competed with his classmates for curricular and extracurricular honors. But during those first twelve years of school, the youngster has had the cozy protection of a family and a home that has made the little races he has run *child's play*.

Then comes the "giant step" . . . graduation. At every commencement ceremony in the land, *somebody* is sure to point out to the happy, wide-eyed graduates the fact that they are on the "threshold of life." Like so many truisms, the reason this one is so often stated is that it is *so true!*

Even though he may be bored by the trite rhetoric of those who so solemnly proclaim the significance of the moment, the average graduate must recognize the truth in it because he has already begun to *feel* the impact of that truth.

By the time he finishes high school, the competition ahead of him has begun to make itself vividly clear to every graduate—whether he plans to go to work, or to go to college. On one hand, he must compete with his contemporaries to get *in* to a job. On the other hand, he must compete to get *in* to a college. In either case, the competition boils down to a measurement of what the graduate has accomplished during the twelve years of his schooling. If he has used his time well, making the most of each experience along the way, his efforts will start paying off for him the moment he leaves high school: jobs are easier to find (and to keep); colleges are easier to get into (and to stay in). For the graduate who has let his time in high school slip by, failing to run the day-to-day race, standing still instead of moving ahead step by step, the first big blow falls when he discovers that he is way behind in a race that started some time ago: jobs are harder to find (and to keep); colleges are harder to get into (and to stay in).

For far too many, it comes as a shock to discover a simple fact-of-life: in the competition that is the muscle of the free way of life, "the race" is actually a tally of points earned in the past. In that first big contest that looks so large at graduation, the points have been earned during the twelve years of schooling that have preceded it; and there is no way to cram enough into the last few months of the senior year to make up for lost time.

To win a race, even to compete with any hope of winning, the competitor must stay "in condition." To be ready with enough points on his side to count, the individual must be in there making those points, day in, day out. It's a steady progression. Either you go ahead with each day's opportunity or you go backward. Standing still is equivalent to going backward; others are moving ahead.

For the young person who wants to go to college, the race is not just a fast sprint to be run at the end of high school.

For the college graduate who wants to get a good job with a future, the race does not begin at college commencement.

It's a long-distance race. The only way to reach the goal is to take it step by step, steadily moving forward.

There is no EASY way.

There is a good way . . . the American way . . . free, healthy competition.

Basically, that is the subject of this book. In each of the chapters that you encounter as you move along through it, you will find that we are discussing the competition you face and the need to make the most of your abilities, your opportunities and your time. Hopefully, you will be better equipped to run the race to your full capacity after you have finished reading these discussions. Before you read ahead, however, let me explain the *reason* behind my writing this book.

You see, I believe that in this day-to-day march forward, this unrelenting competition with your fellow Americans, you can find—if you are able to see them—solid, reliable stepping stones that will lead you forward; make your way easier. And, at almost every turn, most young people have available to guide them qualified "experts" whose job it is to smooth their path and increase their rate of progress. But, much too often, young people do not take advantage of these guiding hands and they fail to see those solid, reliable stepping stones.

Why?

Well, as we have so often heard, "people are funny." They are a lot like horses, if you are to agree with the old maxim, "You can lead a horse to water but you can't make him drink."

People can be led right up to a fact as big as life. There it is, staring them in the face! *But*—if they do not *want* to see it, they don't.

Why?

The answer to that one can become pretty involved; so, let's just settle on a simple word: ATTITUDE.

Our ATTITUDE is like a pair of mental "colored glasses." It colors everything we think. Everything we must evaluate takes on the coloration of our attitude.

When our attitude is clear and uncluttered, the thinking comes out clear and uncluttered. But when we adopt a large set of prejudicial attitudes brought on by experiences that have colored our values, then the thinking comes out phony and mixed up. And the person involved can be so blinded by the color his attitude throws on everything he approaches that he cannot see those solid, reliable stepping stones to lead him forward and he rejects those qualified guiding hands that are extended at almost every turn.

So, that's the reason! That is why I am writing this book.

Essentially, I want to talk to you about those attitudes that get in the way of your progress in this steady, competitive march forward.

As we talk about the various subjects that are the concern of most young people, particularly those who have plans for college, you will see that I bring up some facts to work with. But, for the most part, I have left most of the *facts* about "getting into college" and "choosing your college" and "preparing for college" to the several excellent books that are now available to you.

Then, in the second section of this book, you will find a GLOSSARY of terms which should be of interest to anyone who is going to college. The language in this section is as factual and as concise as I could make it. Whenever I could arrange it, I tried to keep the *facts* for your reference in the second section, reserving the first for our talks about *you, your problems, your attitudes* and the great American *race.*

All set?

Fine. Let's start with a situation that can look bad, but can be fixed if the coloration of a misguided attitude is removed.

BEHIND THE CLASS

REMEMBER when the teacher first asked you to write a "composition" about your favorite pet or your summer's vacation or the story of your life?

Remember your first spelling test?

Or the first time a teacher returned a paper to you with a grade on it?

That's when you began your preparation for college.

By the ninth grade, you began to see how it all adds up.

And by the tenth grade, the chips were down. It's not so easy to catch up after that.

It is not the marks on paper that stand in the way. There is no law or school regulation that insists a student who has made poor grades during the first ten years of school *may* not make good ones the last two years. It just doesn't work out that way very often.

It's all logical, too, when you realize that the brain is a muscle. Like any other muscle in the body, it must be exercised if it is to increase its working capacity. To lift a three-hundred-pound weight, to do a complicated ballet leap or to throw a baseball, you must get your muscles in shape for it. You certainly cannot expect to accomplish it the first time you try.

To understand advanced algebra, to be able to put ideas on paper in a way that will make sense, to concentrate, to study; all these are complicated maneuvers for the brain and they cannot be done by anyone who has not worked his brain up to it. It takes a great deal of *practice*.

During your years in elementary and junior high school, your brain has been put through a systematic set of exercises. Each year, your courses have been designed to build on the learning of the preceding years.

When you put up a tower, you start with the foundation. The taller the tower, the deeper the foundation. No one would consider trying to put the top trim on a building until the base of it is solid.

Yet, high school juniors and seniors try to do it. When the pressure gets tough during the last two years of high school, they "see the light." They make an attempt to change their whole attitude toward school work. With the shaky base of indifferent work during ten grades of foundation studies, they expect to launch into the advanced work of the last two years of high school and to understand what it's all about.

Willingness to work at their studies always helps. Sometimes the grades even improve a little. But the unfortunate fact of the matter is that poor groundwork in mathematics and English composition shows up and slows up any junior or senior who is trying to make up for it with increased effort brought about by his new attitude toward his work. The best way to make up for a lack of understanding of the basics is to go back to the basics and learn them. If the foundation's shaky, fill in the weak spots to make it solid enough to build on.

For the high school junior or senior who has "seen the light" and wants to do better work during his last years than he has done during the earlier times, I have one firm recommendation: talk to your teachers. Ask them to give you achievement tests that will show up your specific weaknesses.

Then, with their help, take review courses, work with a tutor. Use your initiative. Go to summer school. Look around; maybe there's a good fourth-grade teacher who will run you through some of the material you never mastered. You'd be surprised how much they teach in the fourth, fifth and sixth grades—surprised, that is, if you didn't make an effort to get it at the time it was available for you.

Face the logical, simple truth: a willingness to do better is not enough. Most often, the junior or senior who wants to make up for past negligence in his studies simply does not know *how*. He needs encouragement and instruction to keep him on a constructive path. To sit for hours with home-work that makes no sense can do more harm than good. He must learn to walk before he can run, and at all times during his learning he must experience the pleasure and profit of knowing that his effort is getting him somewhere. Even if it's slow, a student who is trying must sense some progress.

I repeat: to avoid spinning your wheels, *get help. Talk to your teachers.*

"Wheel-spinning" is waste. Neither you, as an individual, nor your nation, as a whole, can afford such waste.

We have been talking about the student who is behind the general rating of his whole class. When he tries to do better but does not accomplish anything, it is a waste and he must take steps to correct it. But, unfortunately, the great-est waste that is occurring in our high schools today involves, not the students who are *behind,* but, instead, those who are *ahead* . . . the bright, talented students with higher than average I.Q's.

If you fall into this category, watch out! You may be guilty of a misuse or lack-of-use of a commodity that is very precious to you and to your nation. The next few pages are addressed to you.

AHEAD OF THE CLASS

THINK BACK over your years of schooling. Have you found that you can get your work done in less time than it takes others in your class?

Do your marks stay high although you know you do not spend as much effort on your studies as others do?

Have you found yourself thinking that the teacher is going over material that you already understand?

If so, you are wasting your brain power.

Your teachers and your parents have known of your potential for years. Your aptitude, interest and achievement tests have revealed how much you are capable of doing ever since you started taking them. That's why you have heard so often, "You *could* do *better* if you *tried!*"

In almost every high school today there is a program for the so-called brighter students. The development of this potentially superior brain power is a great concern of the nation, in general; of educators, specifically; and it should be the concern of every bright student and his parents.

Forget for the moment the pressing national need for all the trained young minds available in this country. Think only of yourself. If you have not used your abilities up to their capacity, you have allowed your brain to become lazy or, worse, you have exercised it with non-constructive activities. In either case, you are the loser. During your growth, you are building your own private future. Every ounce of energy you spend in learning, every process of mental activity that you master is some day to be yours to use for your own profit. At no time in your life do you get such full return for your efforts as you do during your schooling period. You are, truly, in business for yourself, with no taxes, no partners; *you* keep all the profits.

Now, if you have been taking the easiest way, getting by without maximum effort, you have been cheating yourself. You should face up to your capacities. Test them to the fullest. Press them with as exciting and advanced school work as you can handle.

Academic programs for students who are ahead of their class vary from high school to high school, region to region. But for the bright student who is seeking a way to get more than is offered to the average student, there is usually a way to find it. In more and more schools, the "enriched" programs provide advanced courses in English composition, mathematics and sciences. The larger the school, the more advanced courses available, naturally; but even in the smallest schools, there are ways to provide a challenge for exceptional students.

To illustrate: your principal can write to the nearest college or university—or to a college or university of your choice—to inquire about available extension courses that will interest you. Talk to your principal about this. You will be pleased at the kind of eager co-operation you will receive.

In addition to the extension courses that have been offered for many years, there is a new source of advanced or enriched courses for the curious and able student. Through educational radio and TV, a number of schools throughout the country are offering classes by kinescope at an hour just before or after school, or sometimes during a special period in the school day. These kinescopes can be shown on a regular 16 mm movie projector and the courses available have a wide and interesting range. There are advanced courses in science, mathematics, languages (Russian, for instance), art, English, public affairs and many others. For information about the courses and the experiences that other schools have had with them, *your principal* (*not you*) should write to: NATIONAL EDUCATIONAL TELEVISION & RADIO CENTER, 2320 Washtenaw Avenue, Ann Arbor, Michigan.

In addition to the filmed courses, there are fine radio educational series available. They may be played back on a tape recorder, which almost every school in the country has these days. Your principal should write for information about these radio courses for advanced students to: THE NATIONAL ASSOCIATION OF EDUCATIONAL BROADCASTERS, 14 Gregory Hall, Urbana, Illinois.

Now, let me make one point very clear: individuals should not request these Radio-TV educational series. They must be secured by the school. Either you or your parents should talk to the faculty of your school about them if you are interested.

If, however, circumstances are such that you are not able to secure advanced work within your school, then you and your parents should consult your school adviser about colleges that allow "early admittance."

"Early admittance" means that, after proper testing, the student who qualifies is allowed to begin his college work before he has graduated from high school. It is designed for the young student who has gained all the education his high school has to offer before he has served the time usually allotted to it.

Some educators and psychologists argue that although a youngster may be ready *academically* for college before he completes his twelve years of school, he is not ready *emotionally*. His social development may not have kept pace with his mental growth.

For the most part, I share this belief. However, I have visited many colleges that allow early admittance, and in my conversations with students who left high school at the end of their tenth or eleventh year, I have heard very few of them say they regretted it. They were young, no doubt about that. (It seemed odd to be talking to college juniors and seniors who were only eighteen years old.) But most of them explained that they felt they were better off than if they had been forced to stay in high school when it had nothing more to offer them. Quite candidly, they admitted that high school had become a bore, academically. There had been no challenge left in the work and they had decided, with the counsel of their parents and teachers, that they should move along to college work.

How much they missed by moving into a social group much older than they is hard to determine. Certainly, they missed something if they were denied the time for social growth that occurs during the last two years of high school. But the young people themselves told me that they had been willing to sacrifice the pleasure and advantages of a more normal social growth for a more important consideration—continued academic challenge.

And that seems to be the crux of the matter: if high school can continue to challenge brighter students, then certainly they are better off staying with their own age group. But if there is nothing left in the high school curriculum that will keep the exceptional student interested and moving ahead, then it is wise to look into early admittance possibilities, on either a part-time or a full-time basis. Whatever steps have to be taken, a bright student should not become bored, treading water academically while he waits for the traditional ceremony of graduation.

One more point: the student who enters into an advanced program should be able to continue with his advanced studies. It is not wise to allow this growing young mind to be exposed to work that challenges him one year and then to follow it the next with average work that will bore him.

For any student who is ahead of his class, I offer this urgent advice: once you enter into an advanced program— no matter at what grade—work with your guidance teachers to see to it that you keep up your progress—even into college.

It is possible for a good student today to take full advantage of an enriched high school program and actually to be doing work at a college freshman level during his high school senior year, then, to be sent off to college and simply be assigned to a regular freshman course. Thus, his progress grinds to a halt. With average level college work, he treads water for a whole year. Any high schol student who enters into advanced work must make it a point to see that his high school notifies his college and recommends his placement in advanced freshman courses. This does not necessarily mean that the student should enter college with *credits;* it often means that he will be placed in advanced *sections* of freshman courses. If the college does not offer advanced freshman sections, then it is not the school for that young mind.

This situation is handled most efficiently by colleges that give *placement* examinations to all entering students. Through these measurements, a college is able to place the student in a section or a course that will use his full capacities. These placement examinations have been standard procedure for the better schools for years; but, unfortunately, there are still too many that do not use them. With the overcrowding of the freshman classes, particularly in state-supported schools, it seems imperative that these institutions set up an efficient system of measuring the capacities of incoming students with a view to making the most of the better ones and giving the poorer ones another chance to catch up.

So far, we have been talking about the small percentage of students in high school who are either behind or ahead of the others. Obviously, the bulk of the students are right where they are supposed to be: in the large middle group. This is the group for whom the major part of the curriculum at a school is designed.

And . . . this is the group for whom the rest of this book is written. From this point forward, I will be talking to the *average* student.

The intention of the talk is to help that student get more out of his work and his life in school—both high school and college.

Let's start with LISTENING. . . .

NOW HEAR THIS!

EACH DAY, when you go to school, you automatically take with you two tools which CAN be among your most valuable assets. For many of you, however, they have long since rusted into ineffectiveness. I am speaking of your EARS.

You still use them. As a matter of fact, you devote far more time to this than to any other activity. But in all probability, you are operating your ears at only about a twenty-five per cent level of efficiency!

It's not that you're hard-of-hearing. Far from it. You're hearing an incalculable amount . . . because there's more to hear . . . and it's coming to you from more places . . . in more ways than ever before in human history.

It's just that you're HARD-OF-LISTENING. And it's only

natural that you would be, from the way things have been going.

Time was when the ear was "top dog" in the learning process. From the beginning, we humans have learned much of what we know by listening. Even before we arrived at communication by spoken language, our ears funneled in many essential clues to living . . . to living well, and, in countless instances, to living at all!

Gradually, to the sounds that betokened sufficiency and survival, there were added the WORDS that carried our facts and thoughts and feelings back and forth, from one person to another.

And for a very considerable span of time, these important messengers came by one route only . . . THROUGH THE EARS.

The youth of the tribe, eager to know, HEARD the accumulated wisdom of the past from their elders. The disciples of Jesus sat at His feet and LISTENED. To the neophyte scholars who gathered within earshot, Socrates, Plato, Aristotle SPOKE the great truths as they saw them.

Then, with the invention of movable type, the words found themselves pinioned upon the printed page, imprisoned for those who wished to come alone and at leisure and to learn by looking. And the more people looked, the less they listened. The more they READ, the less they HEARD. Gradually, reading supplanted listening as the preferred inroad from the fields of knowledge to the minds of men.

The ear . . . ancient, well-used, primary medium of

learning . . . found itself running a poor second to that Johnny-come-lately in educational favor . . . the eye. It was for the new favorite that the printing presses spilled their ever-increasing riches. It was for the good reader that the mushrooming textbooks hoarded the wealth between their covers.

This same pattern, in telescoped form, has happened in your life. It has happened in mine. It is repeated every time a child progresses from the cradle to the first grade. In our first years, we use our ears like magnets to draw in the sounds of language and all the knowledge that oral language has to offer us.

From what is said to us, read to us, sung to us, or overheard by us, we garner the "do's" and "don'ts" . . . the "can's" and "can'ts" . . . the "is's" and "isn'ts" . . . the "why's" and "why not's" that constitute what we know about the world and our place in it as young children. As children, we are LISTENERS. We have to be.

And then we learn to read. Gradually, just as they did in the long reaches of human history, our eyes win out. We become READERS.

And our poor old ears, ignored and unappreciated, retreat in disgruntlement to the sides of our head . . . and just hang there.

The sounds still come. A world of oral communication . . . much of it valuable . . . some of it irreplaceable . . . still presents itself for our attention. But it comes around to the side doors, so to speak. Why? Because most of the mind we have is too busy peeking out the front windows of our eyes.

Finding no welcome, oral communication straggles away, or wanders unattended through the back hall . . . coming in one ear . . . going out the other.

We are simply not listening. At least, we are not listening efficiently. We HEAR, but we don't HEED.

Well, we'd better learn to heed. It's important for all the rest of our learning that we do.

For one thing, we spend almost three-fourths of our waking time in verbal communication. And the giant's share of that time is spent listening . . .

In face-to-face conversation . . .

On the telephone . . .

To the radio . . .

In the movies . . .

To records . . .

To television . . .

AND IN THE CLASSROOM.

Now, there's nothing really new about the fact that, if you're listening ineptly, you're wasting the bulk of your time. This first came to light in a survey made a number of years before you were born. But, new or not, it's unsettling.

And so is the likelihood that you'll waste even more of your time in the years just ahead, because colleges and universities are the natural habitat of the CLASSROOM LECTURE . . . oral communication at its most concentrated. While some teachers slavishly parrot the textbook, the majority use the lecture to supplement, extend and enrich this standard fare. The only way to get such important additional material is to hear . . . and to heed.

Many a student who has mastered the text and other assigned reading has impoverished his grade at the listening post.

Extensive testing of thousands of students and hundreds of business and professional people tells us why.

Immediately after you hear someone talk . . . no matter how carefully you think you have listened . . . if you are the average person you remember only ABOUT HALF of what you have heard. Two months later? Only ABOUT ONE-FOURTH.

But take heart. We're learning some things about listening that can change all this. To cheer you up quickly, here are some of them:

Listening is a skill.

It can be improved with training and experience.

Poor listeners have shown tremendous improvement after such training and experience . . . in special listening classes.

There are such classes, a number of them, in schools and colleges throughout the country. There will be more as time goes on.

And they will be increasingly successful in helping us to heed more of what we hear, because the ear is no longer lying fallow, out of the spotlight. Trained and enthusiastic people who recognize listening as the important learning process it is are hard at work, studying our listening habits and techniques with creative care.

In 1957, a book [1] on listening was published, written by a pioneer in listening efficiency and a consultant in industrial communications. The jacket told us: "This is the first book devoted to a dynamic new science—the science of listening." In it, the writers discussed new techniques of listening, offered tests to establish listening ability, gave information on efficient note taking, gave suggestions for improving the teaching of listening in schools.

Other writings have followed . . . books and articles. Some of them may be available to you through your school or home town library. And they make valuable reading.

From them we learn that a very significant "L" has been added to the three "R's" in education . . .

That emphasis is rapidly swinging back to LISTENING as a primary learning process . . .

That you don't teach people to listen by telling them TO listen . . . but by telling them HOW TO listen . . .

That if you're going to get the most out of your education, wherever you are, you must learn with skill and efficiency to listen . . . understand . . . and remember.

It can be done.

How to is the trick.

To master it, you need that "SECRET INGREDIENT" of all learning processes . . . CONCENTRATION.

Which brings us around to . . . the two ways to Study. . . .

---

[1] *Are you Listening?*, Ralph G. Nichols, Ph.D. and Leonard A. Stevens, McGraw-Hill Book Company, Inc., New York, 1957.

THE LONG AND THE
SHORT WAY . . . TO STUDY

TAKE A typical case. You have four assignments to work out before school tomorrow. There's a theme for English. A chapter to outline for History. A vocabulary quiz in French. And thirty-five dreadful problems in Algebra.

It is almost seven o'clock and you've just sat down at your desk. There's all that homework staring you in the face. You start by opening the History book and while you're moving your eyes down the pages, your mind wanders to the English theme you have to finish, the remark that Jane Doe made in the hall this afternoon, something your father said at dinner, a TV show you're missing, a party that's coming up this week end . . . like flashes on a screen, one leading to another, darting quickly by. All the while, your eyes are moving steadily along the words on the page. Finally, you turn the page and then, as if coming out of a dream, you realize you haven't the foggiest idea of what you have read. You look at the clock; it's fifteen after seven. What happened to the time? You'll never get that homework done! Why do they give you so much to do? How dull can a book be? Ah . . . to heck with history! You'll never get it all done, anyway. You slam the book shut and decide to try the Algebra.

Typical?

Sure, it is. Thousands upon thousands of students are doing much the same thing, night after night.

It's not that they are not willing to spend time at their studies.

The trouble is . . . they *waste* time at it.

Why?

Here it is again! The secret ingredient is missing. There is no CONCENTRATION involved in their efforts to learn.

Yet, take these same students in another learning situation. Each of them has, at one time or another, entered into a learning experience that involved concentration. The girls have learned the words to a popular song or how to knit or to do a new dance step or how to roll up their hair in a new style. The boys have learned tennis, golf, football plays, baseball batting averages. And they couldn't have learned any of them if they had not been able to concentrate.

But, in each case, they applied themselves to one learning chore at a time, and found pleasure in the experience because they *wanted* to learn. It was fun. It was something they *liked,* were interested in.

What's more, their incentive was increased as they became aware of the progress they were making.

On the other hand, *homework.* Four assignments in one night! Dull stuff you have to take just to get out of school. Who needs it?

Without the incentive, without the fun, how can they be expected to concentrate?

Well, actually, they can't be. It is very difficult to force yourself to concentrate against your will. In order to concentrate on anything, you should be drawn to it by a private curiosity or drive. You must *want* to learn it, for one reason or another. And as you learn it, you must derive some satisfaction from your accomplishment.

Now, how in the world are you going to convince students who have difficulty with the dull "stuff of school" that the stuff they call "dull" is *not*. That, actually, they *want* to learn it; and once they start learning it, they will find pleasure in it?

Teachers for generations have been trying to do just that. Each day in some way, they make their point and watch the fire of curiosity come to life in the mind of some student. But always, always, there are those who have managed to keep their minds closed, determined to resist the job of learning anything that is taught in a classroom. These poor, misguided young people have been led to believe that school is something they have to live through, a difficult period every youngster must survive in order to be a grown-up.

Oddly enough, many times they have been misled in this by teachers themselves. Teachers who have failed to communicate any of the joy of learning, any of the excitement of the subject at hand. Other times, the parents of the youngsters are the guilty ones. Unbelievable as it may seem, parents have . . . in far too many cases . . . fostered resistance to learning in their own children. They have gone along with the "popular" concept that teachers are "drags" and school work is a bore. Undoubtedly, these parents are people who never experienced the deep-seated pleasure of learning, of watching horizons broaden as understanding widens, of discovering new personal capacities and avenues of interest.

What a waste!

You see, the truth of the matter is that in every single class . . . no matter what the subject! . . . there is something to learn that you could find *interesting, fun* and . . . (Hold on! You may think I've gone too far, but I'll defend it.) *exciting*.

Now, before you rear up and start calling me some kind of a "nut or something," just let me point out that I do not expect a man who is primarily interested in engineering to get as much pleasure out of a study of Keats' poetry as he does out of courses more directly concerned with his field. Nor could I expect a girl who is a fine painter to find as much excitement in her chemistry class as she does in her Art courses. But . . . I insist that if the girl has an open mind, an uncluttered curiosity, she will find the simple logic, the orderly progress of facts that are presented in the chemistry course a fascinating experience. And in a round-about-way, she may even find that it relates itself to art. As for the engineer, why should he deny himself a chance to look upon any kind of beauty? He can find it in a bridge or any example of engineering mastery; yet it is also in the poetry, if he doesn't close his eyes before he looks. And no man is without a capacity to enjoy beauty; he only has to allow himself to see it.

But we started out talking about the two ways to study . . . the long and the short way. How does all this relate to the subject?

Very simply.

The long way to study is to spend time at it *without* the secret ingredient: CONCENTRATION.

The short way is to get the most out of the minutes you spend through the application of the secret ingredient.

There are, of course, certain techniques of studying that will help. No doubt you have heard of them:

1. Organize your work. Start with your most difficult subject first. Allot more time to the tough one, but do not fail to give some time to each subject.

2. Do not sit at a study table more than an hour at a time. Give yourself five- or ten-minute breaks every hour. Get up, move around, leave the room, clear your mind. Then, before resuming your work, re-

view what you have done so that you keep a sequence in your learning.

3. If the material you are reading is difficult to comprehend, read a paragraph at a time. Do not move to the next paragraph until you have understood the point of the preceding one. It often helps to make summary notes of material as you read it, thereby forcing yourself to put into your own words what you have read.

4. No matter what you tell yourself, a radio or TV set going beside you as you study does NOT help you to concentrate. It is bound to be a distraction. So turn it off. Give your work your *full* attention.

And so it goes. All of the "tips" or techniques for effective *studying* actually are various devices to help you to CONCENTRATE. Without it, you cannot study effectively. Without it, you cannot learn.

With it, you make the most of your time. It's the short way!

With it, you find yourself moving forward. It's the satisfying way!

With it, you begin to see the point of your learning and the whole picture starts to form. It's the fun way!

So, you're sold. You'll concentrate.

Now, how do you learn to concentrate?

It's just as we were saying at the start of these discussions. It's an ATTITUDE, my friend.

Bring to your studies the same attitude you bring to learning how to hold a golf club, a knitting needle, or a winning bridge hand, and you are fast on your way to acquiring the secret ingredient that will open up whole new vistas of pleasure and lead you straight to the short, efficient way to study.

From *studying,* it seems only natural that we should turn our attention to *tests.*

READING, WRITING

AND . . . TESTS!

START WITH five simple, logical facts that you've known
ever since you started to school:

1. When a teacher wants to know if you have understood something he has tried to teach you, he must
   ask you to explain what you have learned.

2. To find out if you have grasped the meaning of a
   reading assignment, he must ask you to state it in
   your own words.

3. When there are more than three or four students
   in a class, a teacher does not have time to admin-
   ister a thorough oral quiz to each one individually.

4. In the learning process, it is necessary to pause periodically to check on your progress, to find out what you have mastered and what you have failed to master. Recognizing your errors and correcting them is a forceful way to learn.

5. To compare the size of several objects, you need a measure that will apply the same standards to each. You would not measure one with a rubber band and the other with a yardstick; a standardized measure is the only way to compare them.

There is no arguing with those facts. They are so obvious anyone must agree with them. And they add up to equally obvious conclusions:

For the teacher, written tests are the only reasonable and practical method of measuring the effectiveness of his teaching and the comprehension of a student's reading.

For the student, written tests are the check points in his learning that allow him to recover facts he missed or errors in his understanding.

In other words, written tests are essential to the teaching-learning process.

Yet, for many students, written tests remain a bugaboo, a painfully unfair measure that is inflicted upon them by unreasonable teachers. Too often, these students are joined by their parents in an attempt to explain away a problem, saying, "Oh, poor Johnny. He could make better marks. He is really a very bright boy. But he's just no good when it comes to taking one of those written tests."

What a waste this is. Instead of solving the problem, these people are looking around it, pretending it's not there. Ninety-eight per cent of these students who bemoan the fact that they seem to show up badly on written tests could lick their problem if they would come to grips with it.

In order to make a written test a full and fair measure of your achievement in learning, you must be able to do two basic things:

One: *Read*
Two: *Write*

Forget for the moment that there is a great deal of pleasure in reading, that there is no surer way to find rich, rewarding entertainment. Look at it from a coldly *practical* point of view. If for the rest of your life your success is going to be affected by your ability to understand what is written on paper, then you had better learn how to read and how to understand what is written on paper. Reading is like any other learned ability: you cannot do it without practice. If you are not one who is going to read voluntarily, then put yourself in a situation that will *force* you to practice reading.

If you can read with ready comprehension, you have mastered the first requirement of taking tests effectively. The second is learning how to write, how to put what you know on paper so that another person can read it and understand what you are saying or *thinking*.

For some, the ability to write comes easier than for others. For a few, it is a talent, just as being able to play a piano or to paint a picture is a talent. But that is another matter. The ability to write well enough to take a test, to fill out an application, to compose a summary, or an intelligent business letter, is an everyday talent that can be learned by the average person if he applies himself. This individual with no particular drive to write for pleasure must therefore learn to write through a systematic series of instructions. Since it is not something he will pick up on his own, he must sit himself down in a class and be taught how to put his thoughts on paper in an orderly, intelligible manner.

All of which is leading up to another simple and obvious conclusion. Since the ability to take tests is a critical one in the life of every literate person; since that ability is based primarily on a person's ability to read and to write; since the average person must learn how to read and how to write through courses taught in school; *then* the courses that teach that ability are among the most important courses in school. Namely: ENGLISH COURSES.

Quite apart from the many aesthetic or cultural reasons

for taking English, concentrating strictly on the practical motivations, I submit that English courses are absolutely essential in high school and that each high school student should take an English course every semester he is in school, whether he is going to college or not. (Actually, for utilitarian reasons, an English course in high school can mean as much to the student who is taking a vocational course as to the student intending to go to college.)

But this could be after-the-fact advice for the high school senior or college freshman who has always had great difficulty with tests. What can you do about a sub-average ability to read and to write when you are a senior and past the time of classroom instruction in the basic skills? I suggest that the student who wakes up to his deficiency in reading and writing should go about learning to read and to write just as he would go about learning to type or to play the piano. (Talk to some friendly faculty adviser. Ask about the basic courses that you can take on your own time. These courses will, if you apply yourself to them, get you on the right track, starting at the beginning. Remembering that any skill takes practice and concentration and the will to learn it, you will find that you are encountering again instructions you heard when you were in the early grades. Now, though, it will make great sense to you, and you will find that it's great to make progress where you've been wheel-spinning.) It is never too late to learn how to read if you genuinely *want* to. The trick is to recognize how important it is. Once you do that, the desire to improve your ability follows quite naturally. Again, *concentration* is the magic word.

And what about writing? Can a high school senior who has always done less well on tests than he should have done simply because he was at a loss to know how to express himself through words on paper improve his ability with words? Of course! It is a skill that can be learned and, as I have said, it does not require any extraordinary talent. The first step in learning how to put thoughts down on paper in an orderly fashion is to read others' thoughts expressed in an orderly fashion. Anyone who reads well has little or no difficulty in expressing himself on paper. Reading develops his ability to think; it increases his experience; it gives him ideas to work from and with; and—most important for the person who is anxious to develop the "knack" of writing clearly— it serves as a means of instruction through illustration.

Now, why am I making such a point of this ability to read and to write in this general discussion of a person's progress through high school and college?

Because I know of no more important point to make.

Every day of your life you will be asked to read something and to understand it. The reading matter could be instructions for filling out an income tax blank, a recipe in a cook book, or a question on a college boards examination. No matter what it is, your day-to-day progress in life will be affected by your ability to read and to understand quickly what you read.

As for writing, there are two vital, practical reasons for being able to put thoughts on paper in an orderly fashion.

First, of course, is the obvious one that we have discussed. If you put your thoughts on paper intelligibly, you will make better marks on tests, fill out applications with more effectiveness, write better letters, and—generally—make a better impression on anyone who has occasion to read what you write. But the second—and, in the long run, more basic—reason for developing the ability to write out your thoughts is that writing well teaches you to think well. After all, writing is the transference of thought from the mind to a piece of paper. Writing *well* is the transference of those thoughts in an *orderly fashion* so that they make *sense* to the reader. To be able to think in an orderly fashion opens the door to an orderly, happy life. Writing is a discipline that teaches you to think. What could be more important to you in your progress through high school and college . . . and *life?*

So having made the point that, in my opinion, English courses should be the hub of everyone's education, let's talk more generally about the course of learning in high school. . . .

THE COURSE OF LEARNING
IN HIGH SCHOOL

I HAVEN'T counted them, but I have been told by people who actually have, that in this country there are more than five hundred different courses taught in our high schools today. Along with these counts, on the other hand, I have never read or heard from any of those people who make a specialty of the matter a listing of precisely which of those five hundred courses are the best ones to take. That is why there are five hundred courses. People vary in their interests and abilities. The world is wide and the scope of the work people are doing in this world gets wider every day; and so, the areas for learning get wider.

As an individual, your course of learning in high school should be fashioned to fit your needs and your interests.

The more carefully you plan that course, the more good you will get out of it. You should start in the ninth grade, working with your teachers and parents to determine which courses will have the most to offer you.

To counsel you in the exact course that is best for you to choose requires professional training and full knowledge of the individual concerned. I have neither. Therefore, on these pages I intend to present only my opinion on generalized attitudes toward the planning of a course of learning. I strongly suggest that if you are interested in the ideas I present, you should discuss them with professionals who know you better than I do.

I believe that it is a great error for any student to abandon a college preparatory course in the ninth grade. Not because I believe that every student should go to college. (I certainly do not believe that.) But because the general academic course is, in my opinion, more effective training for the future than vocational training. In other words, I believe a person who plans to be a craftsman in a vocation will be a better craftsman if he gets as much academic background as he can during the years of his secondary education. He will be able to learn his craft better and progress in his craft further if he has trained himself to think and has given himself something to think with. That, in essence, is the mission of an academic base as opposed to the limited, technical, specialized base offered in the vocational courses. Also, there is always the consideration that when a student is allowed to take a course of study in the ninth grade that will preclude his getting sufficient training to permit college entrance, he is allowed to shut the door to college before he is actually able to be sure of his plans. I see no point in it. Even if a youngster and his parents agree that college is not for him, that a vocation is his very honorable destiny, what good reason is there for closing the door on college and moving the youngster into so restricted a course of study that he puts a ceiling on his potential in his chosen vocation? The academic course, with all the variations now possible in most high schools, has more to offer to any student than the restricted, so-called vocational course.

For those who plan or hope to go to college, I repeat, there are several fine books that will provide you with specific and authoritative guidance as to the course of learning you should follow. I suggest you read them. Also, I suggest again that you talk to your guidance teacher or adviser in high school. And I URGE YOU TO START THINKING AND TALKING ABOUT GOING TO COLLEGE AS EARLY AS THE NINTH GRADE.

Starting with the ninth grade, your marks in school will weigh for or against you when it comes time for the big competition to get into a college. The college you choose will have requirements that should start to influence your selection of courses as early as the ninth grade.

The point I am most anxious to sell you is this one: whatever course you take in high school, be sure it is as difficult as you can handle. The most ridiculous reasoning I can imagine is the thinking of a high school student who will take a course just because it is easy and he knows he can pass it. Who is he kidding? By this kind of thinking he is, in effect, short-changing no one but himself. A course that is easy, so will require no effort on his part, is a course that has little to offer him. Yet he must spend the same amount of his time in class with it as he would with a course that could offer him something. On one hand, he makes a deal to spend his time and get *nothing* in return while, on the other hand, he trades his time and gets *something*. Obviously, anyone who makes this kind of deal does not have much respect for his time; therefore, for himself; therefore, for his future.

I urge you to resist the temptation to take a course just because you can get a mark in it with no effort. Remember, no effort nets you nothing . . . every time.

But let's not slide over the need to make decent marks in your courses. I do not mean to suggest that you should take a course that is so difficult you are able to get nothing out of it. I mean only that you should take courses that are as difficult as you can handle. It is up to you, your conscience, your parents and your teachers to guide your selection so that you are working to your full capacicty, and not beyond it.

With the exception of English, I can make no specific recommendations as to exact courses to take. It is an individual matter and it is one that should be worked out carefully for each individual. But I cannot pass on from this area of discussion without pointing out that, in my experience, I have heard many people say that the few extra hours they spent in high school taking *typing* as an "extra" course were certainly hours that paid great dividends. When it can be arranged so that no more essential academic program suffers, the ability to type can be a valuable asset to anyone. But, before you take it, talk to your teachers and do not let it interfere with more important training.

But now, what about *extra*curricular training?

OUTSIDE OF CLASS

IN ANY discussion of college admittance and the factors that weigh heavily for or against a candidate, the subject of extracurricular activities is sure to come up. When students are involved, it is usually a subjective evaluation. Those who have a heavy extracurricular program must feel that it is in their favor; those who have shied away from activities outside their regular class work necessarily feel that an admittance committee does not pay much attention to anything other than classroom reports.

As the competition for college entrance becames more intense, and more and more families are subjected to that suspenseful period between application and acceptance or rejection, the nation's press fills up with stories and articles about what does or does not count in the race to win one of those precious "tickets" to the freshman class of the chosen college.

With so many opinions rampant about so popular a subject, I decided to conduct an extensive survey before I formed my own. I talked to parents, high school and college students, graduates, teachers, and the people most likely to be authorities: members of the acceptance committees at colleges.

The answers I received were varied, significantly. But the one that seemed to be the consensus of those most qualified to speak was the one that came from the Assistant Director of Admissions for Dartmouth College, Mr. Frank A. Logan. What Mr. Logan had to say is, in my opinion, something that both men and women interested in going to college should find worthwhile. The following was his eloquent reply when I asked him what he considers in the evaluation of an applicant for admission to Dartmouth College:

". . . Speaking only for Dartmouth and without going into any great elaboration, let me simply say this. We are primarily interested in attracting and matriculating those students who show every promise of benefiting from the Dartmouth educational experience, a benefit not only to the student but to the society which he will inevitably serve during his post-college years. Ours is the business of learning, and therefore of primary importance in our deliberations is a candidate's record of intellectual achievements and aptitude as well as his potential for success within the framework of our liberal arts curriculum. The academic factors are largely determined by a candidate's school record, the recommendation from his school, the results of the College Board examinations and other standardized test data. The personal qualities which are sought are not unlike those which are universally held to be of a positive nature and important in any standard personality evaluation. Such traits as independence, maturity, honesty, resourcefulness, etc., are always significant in college admissions. Among these personal qualities, certainly common decency and integrity must inevitably rank high on anyone's list, since no educational institution wants to foster and encourage academic excellence in basically dishonest or evil men. While I am on this particular topic, I can expand upon this business of extra-curricular activities in college admissions, since a great deal on this topic has been in the public prints these days.

"I personally feel that any normal secondary school student who possesses the positive character traits mentioned above will invariably partake in the customary activities and interests associated with the school and the community. Perhaps athletics enjoy some predominance but only because most boys at that particular age level have a natural predilection for physical skills and demands. College is also a community, and a significant portion of the four-year program of learning takes place outside the classroom through means of the various activities offered in the undergraduate campus life. It stands to reason that any responsible admissions officer is also making predictive judgments as to a candidate's promise in this non-academic area of his college experience, and when a secondary school student has acquitted himself well in this or that activity, perhaps even with some distinction, it is a reasonable expectation that he will also be in a position to contribute similarly during his college years, if not afterward. The student who skims the surface, so to speak, and is content to join various clubs simply for a superficial participation in order to compile an impressive list of extracurricular activities is certainly at a disadvantage in any competitive admission situation. My favorite word in this respect is 'depth,' meaning that I personally prefer to see the young man at Dartmouth who has pursued one particular interest or activity beyond the usual expected limitations so that he perhaps actually is a first-rate violinist, a skilled or proven debater, an authority on survival in the woods, or a proficient tennis player. In simpler terms, I would much rather see a man do one thing particularly well than attempting to spread himself over several areas without any real accomplishment."

"Depth" is the word. If you are concerned about making your mark in life, moving ahead, creating a positive pattern, use your abilities, improve them, stretch them through trying. To flit hither and yon, settling nowhere, is the superficial way of life.

When you go to class, make the most of your time. Work at understanding why you are there. There's a lot more satisfaction in that approach, believe me, than in the one that allows you to fritter away your time, resisting any effort to learn.

And when you engage in an outside-the-class activity, participate. Contribute! You will get out of anything you do only what you put into it.

If you adopt this attitude, your extracurricular activity is certain to count in your favor because it all adds up to a person with *depth*. And there is no college in the world that does not want (and *need*) that kind of person in its student body.

From a practical point of view, of course, this attitude necessarily limits the number of activities a constructive person can engage in. There simply is not enough time to devote to a wide variety of out-of-class interests.

Remember . . . when you make that application for admission to college, the only "money in your bank" will be your achievements in any activity into which you have put your most constructive efforts.

Now, let's get down to cases and talk directly about going to college.

FIRST, THE QUESTIONS

THERE IS a kind of "College Fever" spreading through our country today and from the way it sounds to me, as I talk to people, it is not very healthy.

I have sensed in many conversations with students and their parents an attitude that bothers me, because it indicates a set of phony values. Time after time, I hear these people talk about the crowded colleges and the competition for college admission, and much too often I realize as they are talking that their primary concern is simply to get *in.* *Staying* in or *learning* something while in college do not occupy their attention nearly so much as the major achievement of getting *in.*

Recognizing the traditional "American" personality, I can

see how this disturbing attitude has grown. It is a result of the same "keeping-up-with-the-Jones" idea that has sold so many automobiles, dish washers and fur coats. But when it is applied to education, this attitude seems even more fool-hardy, and much more wasteful.

Just because everybody else in your class is trying to do it or because everybody else's son and daughter are "going away to school" is not reason enough to think that you, too, must get into a college. To find college desirable only because the demand is greater than the supply is superficial thinking, based on false values, and it will lead you nowhere.

In the discussion that you will encounter in the next few pages, I intend to investigate with you a procedure that you may follow in preparing yourself for college admission. The first step in that preparation—and a very important one—is a thorough analysis of your motives.

Why do you want to go to college?

What do you intend to get out of college?

Is college the best place to get what you need for your life as you intend to lead it?

Now, these are not simple questions. A great many college students could not answer them satisfactorily, even after they have finished the four years of college. Of course, these graduates would be the ones who got little or nothing out of their four years and they are the ones who should serve as an example to you—an example, that is, of what *not* to be. That is the whole point of asking yourself those three questions at the very outset of your planning. If you are going to get nothing significant out of your college training, why spend the time and the money?

I am not prepared to answer the questions for you. Neither are your parents or your teachers. The student who decides to go to college is the only one who can answer them. If you want to go to college, you must know *why*. It must be *your* motivation that guides you in your decisions about (1) going, (2) when to go, and (3) what to do after you get there.

So, from this point on in our discussion, I will operate on the assumption that you have answered the three big questions to your own satisfaction and you are seriously interested in going to college for valid, intelligent reasons.

So, on to #2. *When* to go.

WHEN TO GO TO COLLEGE

IN A FEW words, you should go to college when you are *ready* to go.

That does not necessarily mean the moment you graduate from high school, because, first of all, at that moment you may not be ready *financially*.

College is an expensive proposition. Even if your parents have been saving money for years to pay for your college education, they may find that the costs have gone up faster than the balance in that savings account. So, you owe it to yourself and to your family to go into a financial huddle on the matter. All you need is a pencil, some paper and some realistic facts. A ready source for those facts about a great number of colleges will be found in *The College Handbook,* published by the College Entrance Examination Board. Your school librarian can tell you how to get this handy book. If the college in which you are most interested is not included in the *Handbook,* you can get a catalogue with all the pertinent information in it by writing directly to the school.

Now, put down your tuition and fees, cost of room and board, cost of clothes and incidentals, cost of social life (and do not kid yourself about this item; it definitely figures in the cost of college), cost of travel, cost of medical care and allowance for emergencies. When you think you've listed everything that is required, total it up, multiply by four (if you plan a four-year course), and subtract what you think you might be able to earn with part-time and summer work. When you reach that final figure, ask yourself and your parents if that kind of money is available. If it is not, investigate the possibilities of partial scholarships. (Each year, in every state in the Union, there are scholarships available that are not used, simply because some needy student did not know about them and did not apply for them.) Talk to your teachers and get some help on this. It may take a lot of letter-writing, but it is worth it if you are ready to go to college and only money stands in your way.

Most colleges and universities will tell you they prefer students who have at least enough money before they start to carry them through the first two years. The schools are not afraid of losing money; they are more concerned with losing students. And the casualty rates increase when lack of funds causes mental anguish or forces students to overdo the employment angle.

So much for the *financial* aspect of being ready to go.

The far more important aspect is your *attitude*. Are you ready to enter into the kind of serious learning experience that college should be? Are you going to approach that first year at college as something more than a "13th grade"?

Again, *you* are the only person who can answer those questions.

Of course, you should talk to your parents and your teachers about your plans. And . . . if ever in your life you approach a problem with candor and complete honesty, make it this time.

Remember, you have already answered *the* question. You know that you *want* to go to college, that college training is what you need to equip yourself for your life ahead. The point now under consideration is *when*.

I submit for your consideration the opinion that, for a great many young people, it is wise to spend a year or two between high school and college. To spend that time "growing up" so that the four years of college will net four years of learning what college is designed to teach. In my experience, I have come to know many fourth-year college students who wake up in their senior year and realize that they have wasted most of their first two or three years in college simply because they had not allowed themselves time to mature enough to appreciate what they were there for.

Whenever I have discussed this problem with college

professors, the example of the GI students after World War II comes up. As you know, a great many veterans availed themselves of college benefits through the so-called "G.I. Bill." These men came back from a two-to-five-year period in military service, two to five years "away from the books," as the saying goes, and they proved themselves to be remarkable students. As a group, they compiled a truly amazing academic record. Now, many theories have been advanced for this, but most educators seem to be of the opinion that returning veterans had the stuff to make good in college because they were older and wiser than their predecessors. In a sense, they had *grown up* before they became college freshmen. Colleges and universities found a great many serious-minded, mature young men on campus, and their attitude was quite different from those happy youngsters who had come to the campus thinking that the freshman year was a "13th grade."

The point is simply this: if you decide, for one reason or another, that you are not *ready* to go to college the moment you graduate from high school, the time you spend in between the two learning experiences will very likely make you a better student and will allow you to get more out of your years in college.

Now, I know this is a point of view not shared by many parents and some teachers. And I submit it only as my personal opinion. I realize that in many instances the rush to get admitted to a college causes families to push their youngsters along into higher education while the doors seem to be open. On the other hand, more and more fine schools are recognizing the need for maturity in their students and they have set up a system of "furloughs," whereby a student may be allowed to drop out of school for a period of time and then return with no penalty. This seems to imply that these same colleges would be most sympathetic to a student who has been admitted but who feels he must wait a year or so to mature before he actually starts his education on campus.

Oddly enough, in my experience, the people who have been most vocal about the need to "grow up" before entering college have been college seniors or recent graduates. Those years wasted as a result of not being ready are vivid to them, and they still feel the sting of regret for missed opportunities.

Of course, there are many reasons for moving on ahead with your education while you are still young, keeping up the momentum you have going for you right out of high school. Granted, there is always the danger that you may never get to college if you take out a year or two. (Although I believe anybody who wants to go will only want to go more after he has had some time "out in the world" to see how truly valuable a college education can be.)

And, above all, let me make it clear here that I believe there are a great many young people graduating from our high schools today who are prepared in every way for the experience of higher education. More each year, thank goodness!

The point only is that YOU must be sure that you are *ready* and you must not be pressured into believing that the time to be ready is the year after high school, or *never*. It may very well be one, two, three, four years after you get that diploma. Just be sure before you go that you are old enough to appreciate what college has to offer the student who is there to get full value in return for his effort.

So much for *when* . . . let's move along to *where*.

WHICH COLLEGE
TO CHOOSE

NOW HERE'S a subject about which many articles, books
and all manner of advice have been written.

It is a very big problem and I suggest you read as much
as you can about it. On these pages, I hope to point out the
chief factors you and your family should evaluate. For more
detailed information, I refer you to the other books on the
subject that you will find readily in your school library.

Recognizing that the financial angles of your choice have
already been weighed and are not a factor in the considerations, I submit the following for your guidance:

1. It is wise to select at least three colleges for which
   you are making application. One should be a school

that has an academic standard which will cause you to strain your capacities and for which you will have to meet serious competition to gain admittance. Another should be one with somewhat less critical academic requirements. And the third should be one in which you are reasonably sure of gaining admittance.

2. Consider carefully the size of the college. For some students, a big school in or near a large city has a great deal to offer; for others, the big community is a definite disadvantage. For some, a small college in a small community is a much happier situation and will prove to be a more fruitful learning environment; on the other hand, there are many individuals who will find this kind of college inadequate and frustrating. It all depends upon the personality and background of the student. You, along with your teachers and your parents, should decide what is best for you and then limit your search for schools to either the small or the large variety.

3. The distance from home is another factor to be weighed. Apart from the financial considerations, the location of a college is important. For some young people, it is a good idea to go to school in another part of the country; for others, it is wise to stay nearer home. In this matter, parents should

have a large voice in the decision. Know yourself well enough to have an attitude toward this aspect of your college choice but, at the same time, be prepared to listen carefully to the advice of your parents in this regard. They might know you better than you know yourself and can guide you wisely and well when it comes to this decision.

At this point, we could move along to a lengthy discussion of the frightening prospect of being turned away from the college of your choice. It happens to a great many young people every year. And as the competition for college admittance gets more rigid, it will be a problem for more and more aspirants. It is a complex problem. Colleges throughout the country are faced with it, and steps are being taken to do something about it. It is aggravated by the very fact of multiple applications. With every student applying to three or more colleges, of course each college is going to have more applications than it can accept. With more and more students eager to attend, naturally, the facilities are going to be strained. And so the chances that you will not be admitted to the first college you apply to are greater every year. You must be prepared for a turndown. And it is not easy to take, no matter how well prepared you are for it. However, you must also believe that you will be admitted to *some* school and you must be prepared to believe that the school you finally enter will turn out to be *the* school for you.

In this connection, let me tell you about the actual experiences of some of the "Varsity Scholars" who have appeared on the "G.E. College Bowl" television program with me. These young students are selected by their schools to be members of the "College Bowl Teams" because they are *top* students. Time after time, I have learned from these fine young scholars that they were turned down by other colleges and the one that they were at that moment representing on a nationally televised program was their third or fourth choice. But were they sorry? Never! In all cases, they bore out my theory that whatever school you finally select . . . or that finally selects you . . . will turn out to be the school you most wanted to attend. There is an opportunity for learning in every college in the country. So, keep that in mind, and let it guide you through the disappointment of being turned away from the schools that are too crowded to accept you.

As I mentioned earlier, there are many fine books that will help you in the difficult matter of choosing a college. These books treat the problem in great depth . . . far more completely than I have attempted to do here. But there is one aspect of choosing a college that I did not find discussed in detail in any of the better-known books on the subject.

It is the very important aspect of HOUSING.

And so, let us look into that problem.

Next page, please.

HOUSING

HEADLINES in the local paper proclaim: "Coed Housing Drouth Exists."

The Dean of Men shakes his head as he takes the frantic long-distance call.

The housemother replaces the "Student Rooms and Meals" sign with "No Vacancies."

It all adds up to one thing.

NO ROOM.

This is August, say. Or May. Or April. Or even February. You don't need a room till next September.

You're still too late. There hasn't been a room available in any of the approved college or university housing units or facilities since last October. Sometimes even before that.

61

And though the new dorm MAY be completed in time for the fall semester, or a few new houses for men open up, or a few approved rooms for girls appear somehow or other, you're not much better off if you've JUST BEGUN to think about housing. Priority goes to those two hundred avid supplicants already firmly entrenched on the waiting lists.

The plain truth is that you must be not only foresighted but farsighted about your living arrangements at the school of your choice, or you may find yourself domestically "out," even though you are academically "in."

THE FACT THAT YOU HAVE SATISFIED THE ENTRANCE REQUIREMENTS OF YOUR PREFERRED COLLEGE OR UNIVERSITY AND HAVE BEEN ACCEPTED FOR ADMISSION DOES NOT GUARANTEE YOU A PLACE TO LIVE.

And with no place to live, YOU CAN'T GO.

Unfortunately, the number of men and women wanting a college education has outrun the academic facilities of higher education, and living accommodations are panting even farther behind.

Because of less stringent "approval" regulations for male students, the shortage of rooms for you men is not so acute as that facing you women. And there are, of course, some campuses with space to spare.

But, by and large, in the bigger, stronger and better colleges and universities, housing is at a premium, and reservations must be made (on campus after campus) at least a year in advance, sometimes more . . . sometimes TWO!

Consequently, you cannot decide at the last minute that

a certain university is for you, or that it's high time you got moving with that letter about dormitory reservations. You've got to make these decisions back a year or so before that high school diploma comes your way.

Think ahead about housing, from several standpoints, one being, the kind of housing you feel you'd prefer.

The place where you live, the type of housing you choose, is very important to you. For a semester at least, probably a year, possibly longer, it will constitute your most immediate and ever-present college environment.

You're wise if you give careful thought to making it the best environment possible. To do this, you have to take YOU into account.

Accustomed to a room of your own, with control of the study climate largely in your hands? You may be concerned that the close quarters and noisy congeniality of a dormitory will bother you. Lots of people there. More than in a rooming house, say. And more in a rooming house than in a home near the campus where you may rent a monastic single room.

But possibly you're a convivial soul who feels that solitude is a sentence instead of a gift. Or an iron-minded marvel who can concentrate right through all the bedlam some frenetic folks (families or friends) can produce.

Whatever you are, bear it in mind, and try for the most congenial housing situation you can manage.

Dig deep into the housing rules and regulations of the school that appeals to you. Don't let the fact that it's an academic gem blind you to housing that COULD drive you wild and hamstring your scholastic abilities. One campus, for instance, houses *all* girl students in one outsize dormitory. No sorority houses. All chapters have special dorm wings. Some campuses have only cottage housing. Some depend largely on townspeople to put a roof over students' heads.

Any one of these situations could suit you to a "T." Or it could set your whole personality on edge. Just make sure you know what the situation is.

If possible, test for "housing climate." Not air-conditioning. Attitude-conditioning. Is it a gay-blade place that puts a premium on play and labels every sincere student undesirable? Is it a grim, Wuthering Heights-type, with no concern about relaxed atmosphere, comfort or vitality in living? Or is it a sound, but stimulating, environment that promises to nourish all the best potentials of the people who live there?

Learning is a multi-faced thing, done best in an environment congenial to the learner. Academic programs are important. They constitute your primary consideration. But don't leave housing out of your evaluation in selecting the school for you.

What is your financial situation? Money's-no-object . . . pinch-the-pennies . . . or somewhere in between? There are varying levels of housing costs. (On one campus, for instance, dormitory rooms range from $10 to $50, the latter air-conditioned.) Try to find the level that suits your circumstances without too much strain.

Check on distance from the campus and remember to consider transportation facilities and costs.

Likely, you'll have a choice of:

> DORMITORIES (some university-owned, some privately-owned)
>
> ROOMING HOUSES (you'll have to find your meals elsewhere)
>
> BOARDING HOUSES (meals only)
>
> ROOMING AND BOARDING HOUSES (offering room and a varying number of meals)
>
> FRATERNITY AND SORORITY HOUSES
>
> CO-OPERATIVE HOUSES
>
> CLUBS

Sometimes you will be permitted to live in PRIVATE HOMES (other than your own) and in APARTMENTS. Except in special cases, these accommodations are usually permitted only to juniors and/or seniors or graduate students.

On some campuses, undergraduate students are required to live in dormitories.

On the majority of campuses, undergraduates are required or strongly urged to live in approved houses.

And there are, of course, commuting campuses, particularly in large cities, where housing is left entirely to the discretion of the individual.

The probability, though, is that you won't be living by yourself. Even if you have lone-wolf tendencies, this can be good. Dormitories and the other places where students live give you a chance to develop your social as well as your academic side. You'll have a chance to know all kinds of people, work with them, live with them, LEARN FROM THEM. No, this isn't a saccharine concept. You'll be doing a lot of that in the years ahead. This is a good place to learn the ropes. You'll do yourself a favor if you plan deliberately to make this experience part of your higher education.

Some food for thought:

Tantalizing as the idea of an apartment is to some of you "on-my-own" specialists, remind yourself that the best grades are made in dormitories, the poorest in apartments. It's a fact, confirmed by recent studies. Don't try to convince yourself . . . or your parents . . . that your grades will rise in proportion to the rent.

Fraternity and sorority house living can be an attractive proposition, but be prepared for significantly higher cost and social involvement. (*More later on this.*)

And speaking of costs, a good chance for budget living on campus is often offered by co-ops, or co-operative residences. They are what the name implies. Residents do all the work except, in most cases, cooking. You'll be called upon for a special job assignment (house manager, food buyer, house maintenance, maybe, and these may rotate), in addition to keeping your own room. It means an investment of four to five hours a week of your time, but it can mean room and board some $25 to $30 a month cheaper than in a regular dormitory.

So, here you are, a year or two before you're actually packing your clothes, ready right now to take the first constructive steps toward assuring a roof over your head when you and some college have accepted each other.

Pick out several schools that seem desirable and feasible for you. Write to each one (to the Registrar, or the Dean of Student Life, or the Dean of Men, or the Dean of Women, or the Director of Housing) and request information on living accommodations. BE SURE TO GIVE SOME SIGNIFICANT CLUES ABOUT YOURSELF, YOUR CIRCUMSTANCES AND YOUR PREFERENCES. Request specific facts and recommendations. Don't hesitate to ask direct, concrete questions, as many as you can think of.

Be sure to get clear instructions about housing applications and contracts, about deposits and forfeitures, and the circumstances under which you can change housing arrangements if you want or need to do so.

How you proceed next will depend upon the situation at the school or schools of your choice. Some students prefer to make room deposits at several schools, two at least, if housing shortages on those campuses are acute. This is good insurance and not too risky, financially, as most schools permit cancellation of a room reservation by a given date without forfeiture of deposit. And you may also withdraw from the waiting list without forfeiture if you do so by a specified date, usually about a week subsequent to the reservation cancellation deadline.

Although housing contracts in university-approved residences are generally made with the specific residence, through its director, or manager, or housemother, it is customary for the university to furnish the contract forms and to supervise the contractual performance, enforcing the contract for those on the approved list.

In some instances, contracts are made for one semester only. Moves can be made at mid-year with proper notice. Deposit will be forfeited only if notice is not given by a stipulated time.

You may find, however, that you must make a nine months' contract, and that it either (1) can be broken under certain circumstances, or (2) cannot be broken at all without forfeiting your deposit.

Deposits vary, but most fall into the span from $20 to $40 for the nine months.

In most universities, men do not have regulated hours for checking in to the residence. You women, however, will have regular check-in hours in almost every instance; perhaps eleven or twelve o'clock at night on weekdays, later on week ends or for special events.

If you have looked ahead, planned carefully and given yourself one or two alternative choices of schools, there is every reason to believe that you will have adequate and congenial housing waiting for you when you arrive on campus.

Your room deposit will have been made and YOUR RESERVATION WILL HAVE BEEN CONFIRMED IN WRITING by the proper person. Be sure you know who this is. ACCEPTANCE OF YOUR DEPOSIT IS NOT A GUARANTEE OF HOUSING. It will be returned to you if no housing is available. Do not assume that you have a reservation UNLESS YOU HAVE BEEN PLAINLY TOLD IN WRITING THAT YOU HAVE IT AND WHAT IT IS!

Customarily, unless you have been otherwise instructed, when you arrive on campus you will go directly to the residence unit where your room is reserved.

If this is a dormitory, you will need to check in first at the office or information desk or at the registration desk, which is usually provided in the foyer or living room or one of the rooms near the front entrance.

There you will follow the procedures which are explained to you, probably paying deposits for electrical appliances, receiving instructions for dormitory living, in some instances obtaining permission slips for your parents to fill in. These usually apply to week ends off campus, dating situations and the like, if you are a freshman girl.

This is where you may also receive special information brochures concerning special aspects of the campus, if this material has not been mailed to you prior to arrival.

Customarily, the charges for room and/or board will have been paid in advance, unless you have made special arrangements with the proprietor. The length of periods covered by advance payments varies according to the accommodations selected. Be sure to have with you your receipt for charges paid previously or your letter of confirmation on your room reservation.

When registration procedures at the dormitory are completed, you will be assigned to your room and given instructions as to the most expeditious way of moving your bags and other belongings into the dormitory.

Console yourself that you are not the first freshman ever to arrive on campus. Most of your confusions and puzzlements will have been anticipated and care taken to make your entrance into campus and dormitory living as easy and pleasant as possible. But there may be some things you need to know that nobody has told you.

ASK.

And don't feel foolish about asking. Experienced and poised people make inquiries. It's only the immature and unsure who feel they have to pretend they know.

The canny newcomer pleasantly, but persistently ferrets out what he or she needs to have in the way of information.

Of course, that means you. You were smart enough to provide for your housing in advance, weren't you?

(As I said a few pages back, this subject of Housing is one that seems to be missing from most books on College-choosing; hence, I've gone into it more in detail and taken it further than I would have otherwise.)

Now, back at the high school . . . College Boards!

THE COLLEGE BOARDS

THE College Entrance Examination Board publishes a booklet that will provide you with a complete description of the organization, services and programs of the Board. It is entitled *The College Board Today,* and is available to you if you will write to the College Entrance Examination Board office, 475 Riverside Drive, New York 27, New York. I suggest you get the booklet, study it and take advantage of the understanding it can give you. Knowing what a test is and how it serves you makes taking that test a great deal easier. So, understanding the College Boards is an essential part of your preparations for them.

The one test you are sure to encounter if you take the College Boards is known as the SAT. That stands for Scholastic Aptitude Test. The purpose of the test is to measure your ability to do college work. This particular test has been part of the Board's program since 1926, and ever since 1942 it has been the main testing instrument of college admission for Board member colleges. It is an objective test, the multiple-choice kind of test that you have taken ever since you started to go to school. It is scored on a scale that ranges from 200 to 800. This same scale applies to everyone who takes the SAT, no matter where he lives or where he has gone to school. You see, it is, in fact, a steady measure that can be of great help to college admission officers and to high school guidance teachers.

All colleges that use the College Board measurement, either as official requirements for admission or as unofficial evidence of an applicant's ability, will expect you to take the SAT. Many colleges—and their number is growing every year—also require that you take the Achievement Tests. These tests measure your knowledge of specific subjects. They are one-hour objective tests and candidates usually take one to three of them during the administration of a test. (They are given on the day after the SAT.) Currently, the Board offers Achievement Tests in the following subjects: Social Studies, Intermediate Mathematics, Advanced Mathematics, French, German, Spanish, Latin, Italian, Greek, Biology, Chemistry, Physics and English Composition. There are also Listening Comprehension Tests in French, German and Spanish; and, for students in the Physical Science Study Committee Program, special Achievement Tests in Physics.

In the booklet I mentioned earlier, the Board explains that "the Achievement Tests are developed to reflect, as far as possible, what is being taught in secondary schools, and at the same time to show whether students are prepared for the work they will be expected to do as freshmen in college." Now, as I pointed out, there are still colleges that do not require Achievement Tests; for many, the SAT is all that is required. But even if the college for which you are preparing does not require you to take the Achievement Test, I strongly recommend that you do take the tests in English, Mathematics and one other course of your choice—if for no other reason than to check your own progress in the subjects. No college would refuse to look at the results of your test, and to have had the initiative to take it, although it was not required, should mitigate in your favor in the mind of any admissions committee. But, quite apart from that consideration, the fact that the Achievement Tests give your teachers some measure for your guidance is reason enough to take them.

Taking the Achievement Tests, whether or not they are required, is also a good idea because they are likely to give your morale a boost. I have known young people who shied away from these tests because they were afraid that the results would reveal a disastrous weakness in a given subject. And then, upon taking them, these same students have discovered that they were better grounded in the subject material than even their high school teachers had led them to believe. Given the confidence of knowing that they could master the work in a subject, these students proceeded to move along in that subject with greater efficiency.

(At this point, it might be well to introduce this thought for your consideration. The College Boards can build your confidence in your ability as a student, as well as tear it down. If you are one who is afraid to take the tests because you have a secret fear of a low score, you are only normal. But if you fail to take the tests because of that fear, you are a coward and you are cheating yourself. Isn't it better to know where you stand from the start, so that you can correct your weaknesses or build on your strengths? If you are conscientious enough to be afraid of a low score, there is a very good chance that you are a better student than you think you are. The results of your tests may surprise you. You may have potentials you have been afraid to dream of. Or, on the other hand, you may have been kidding yourself and your teachers. In either case, you are ahead if you find out the truth.)

As we have discussed previously, the need to begin your specific course of action in the direction of college around the ninth grade is becoming more and more self evident as the competition for college admittance grows more rigorous. With more and more ninth- and tenth-grade students approaching their work with college in mind, a need has developed for a kind of measurement that will determine their progress and help their guidance teachers in steering their course. This need was filled in 1959 when the Board made available a new test, a two-hour version of the SAT. It is called the Preliminary Scholastic Aptitude Test (known as the PSAT).

This test is built along exactly the same lines as the SAT, using multiple-choice questions and measuring verbal and mathematical abilities. The scores range from 20 to 80, paralleling the 200–800 range of the SAT.

Talk to your teacher about the PSAT. In many cases, it is possible to take it in the spring of your tenth grade. If you are able to do so, it is a good idea. If you wait until your eleventh grade to take it, that is fine also. The Board has found that the results of these Preliminary tests are excellent measures of a student's college potential. Also, the PSAT serves as a fine "dry-run" for the more important SAT that you will take during the following year or so.

There is yet another reason for taking the Preliminary test. By committing yourself to this test through your application for it, you are gearing your sights to a learning challenge a year ahead of the SAT. The sooner you start with specific objectives in mind, the better equipped you will be. Your teachers and your parents will have a measure with which they can work, and you will have a whole year to prepare yourself more efficiently for the SAT.

I urge you to take the Preliminary Scholastic Aptitude Test if you can arrange it.

While we are on the subject of preparing yourself for the SAT, let me lay to rest some old and vicious ideas about "cramming" for College Boards. No matter what you have been told, forget it. You are wasting your time and your energy on last-minute wholesale studying. It would do you a lot more good to get a full night's sleep.

The Boards are *objective* tests. To answer the questions correctly, you must know how to read accurately and to think in an orderly fashion. You cannot learn that with cramming. To repeat the point I made earlier, to be able to read and to think in an orderly fashion, you must have worked at it systematically over the period of years you have been going to school.

A tutor at the last minute will not help you either. He cannot teach you in a few days how to read and how to write. You must go back to the basics and learn them; to wait until January of the senior year to start catching up is to watch the parade pass you by.

The College Boards are also very difficult for the student who has made his marks in school through muscle-bound memorizing and rote-learning. The very nature of the tests requires an ability to think out a problem. The way to develop that ability is through self-disciplined study and thinking habits. (And you can't pick that up with a few nights of cramming.)

You have also heard, no doubt, that it is possible to be coached in preparation for the College Boards. This has been a matter of concern to the College Entrance Examination Board, and to give you an authoritative statement on the subject, may I quote from the 57th Report of the President of the Board:

"The third of a series of efforts to determine the vulnerability of the SAT to intensive coaching conducted with the sole purpose of improving the candidates' scores indicated, as had the previous studies, that the effects of coaching are negligible. The effects were measured by Robert E. Dear in terms of group performance on two comparable forms of the SAT, one administered before and the other after a program of intensive coaching. It was noted that large score differences were recorded for individuals within the experimental or coached group, but it was also observed that differences of similar magnitude were observed within the second, or non-coached group of students."

That statement from Frank Bowles, quoted above, is the shorter one contained in the report. I have also read the full statement of the Trustees on test coaching, and I can assure you that the more detailed story makes it even more clear that coaching for the sole purpose of improving your SAT score is a waste of time. The results of such coaching do not "yield gains in scores large enough to affect decisions made by colleges with respect to the admission of students."

With this kind of evidence before you, it seems logical that you should abandon any idea of undergoing coaching with the sole purpose of improving your scores on the College Board tests. But if legitimate coaching with qualified teachers is available to you, I suggest you consider taking it.

Granted, your scores will not improve perceptibly. But this "coaching" might serve as an intensive course in how to study under pressure; and you may benefit a great deal from it; if not immediately, later. This, of course, does not apply to all students; and, again, I suggest you follow the advice of your guidance teacher.

Now, to get back to the College Board tests, let's examine the mechanics of the testing procedure. The Board offers examinations at different times during the year. SAT administrations are scheduled for December, January, February, March, May and August. The Achievement Tests are given in December, March, May and August. Special arrangements are made for students with special requirements.

Both the SAT and the Achievement Tests are offered at some fourteen hundred centers throughout the United States and in forty foreign countries. If a student must travel more than seventy-five miles to a center, a special center is established for his convenience.

The results of your tests are sent to the three colleges you list as your choice and to your high school. The high school may tell you the scores you have made on the tests, and I believe you should know the scores. (There was a time when the student did not learn his score, but that has been changed; and I believe it is an improvement in the testing procedure.)

You realize, of course, that on these tests there is no passing or failing. Each college sets its own standards, based on the experience that institution has had with the ability of former students to do the work required of them in that particular school. The score 800 is perfect; and, like all things perfect, very rare. The score of 600 is usually considered good. The degrees of excellence range down from there.

There is much more to know about the College Boards. I repeat, you should talk to someone on the faculty of your high school and learn as much as you can about these tests . . . how you apply for them . . . the costs . . . the nearest center . . . dates for the administration in your area . . . and all other details. Also, to repeat because it is important, secure the booklet offered by the College Entrance Board. Then, with the help of a faculty member, get a copy of the College Handbook for you and your family to consult about the various colleges.

Before we leave this discussion, may I make one point very clear, however? (It is, incidentally, a point also made by the Board in their booklet.) The scores you make on the Preliminary Test, the SAT and the Achievement Tests are only a part of the evidence a college considers when you are applying for admission. Nobody was ever admitted to a good school with high Board scores and a poor scholastic record in high school. Your marks in high school remain the chief factor for consideration by the admissions committee.

Next on the agenda—the question of what to study, once you get to college . . . the big problem of "the Major" and "the Minor."

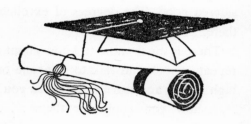

IS COLLEGE ONLY "A WAY TO GET A JOB"?

LET'S GET one thing straight right at the start of this discussion: making up your mind to *go* to college is one thing; deciding *what you are to do* after college is another. It is essential to feel the need for more education if you are to get anything out of the time you spend on your college courses, but it is not necessary to know so precisely what your life work is to be that you head straight for a specific course of study.

A great many young people enter college without a particular major in mind; and believing that the choice of a major is the same as a choice of a life work, this lack of decisiveness becomes a real personal problem for these students. A creeping fear that they are destined for failure because they can't make up their minds about their course of study turns into serious self-doubts. Looking around, they see their contemporaries heading straight for careers in medicine, engineering, teaching, law, etc. And yet, for them, these professions seem to offer no magical attraction. The private fear of failure builds up each time a well-meaning relative or friend tries to get them to decide upon a career. In my opinion, this is all a great mistake.

There is no reason in the world why a young person should entertain self-doubts just because he does not have a specific job in mind when he begins college training. *Most* freshmen do not know precisely what they intend to do after college. The ones who do have a clear-cut course ahead of them are the rare ones. And not always the wise ones.

In the past few decades, the attitude toward specialized training at the undergraduate level has begun to change. And high time!

Even the most technical professions now recognize the value of a broad liberal arts base as a foundation for future specialized training. Technical institutes are encouraging their young students to take as many courses in the humanities as they can during the first years of their college work. No longer is an English major considered an odd ball who will be equipped for nothing in particular when he graduates. Industry and professional groups have realized that the human being who has encountered the great ideas by which man has survived and progressed is very likely to be a person with a capacity for growth in today's society, an ability to deal efficiently with ideas that become reality and mold our way of life. It is no longer a far-fetched possibility for a young man to major in philosophy and to move along to engineering in his graduate studies. It is a very fine base for engineering, as a matter of fact.

All of which should be a consolation for the freshman with no specific major in mind and a note of caution for the student who is driving straight ahead with his sights on one single career or profession. With his sights so firmly set, he runs the risk of training himself too narrowly for that career if he orients his whole course of study to that one objective. Very often the individual who simply does not know what he wants to be and therefore is free to explore the broad vistas open to him through higher education gains a more useful training in the long run.

That is, *if* he explores the broad vistas. On the other hand, if a young person without a strong drive in any one direction seizes upon one of the so-called "professional" majors just so he will be able to get a job when he gets out of college, he may very well find himself with a narrow, empty kind of training and a college diploma that is little more than a union card.

These so-called professional majors are, in far too many cases, a snare and a delusion. I am referring to such established institutions as the "Journalism" major, the "Radio-TV" major, the "Drama" major, the "Speech" major. What I am about to say may raise some eyebrows, and I hasten to add that I am stating only my own opinion. (But

I must also point out that I have talked with many educators who share my feelings on the matter.)

I believe it is a mistake to offer such courses as a major field of study at the UNDERgraduate level. As graduate courses, they have an obviously valid reason for existence. But during the first four years of an individual's college training, he should not be allowed to spend his time for academic credit on matters that are so purely technical. The college diploma is NOT a union card, and no one should spend four years in college simply to facilitate getting a job at the end of the time. (You can get *a job* without a college education.)

Certainly, there should be courses offered in RADIO-TV, JOURNALISM, SPEECH, DRAMA, etc. But they should be available as minors for students majoring in more fundamental fields of study. Also, on each campus there should be active extracurricular activities in these fields that will attract the out-of-class energies of undergraduates in all departments, allowing them experiences with the technical aspect of the field without taking class time to teach them.

To illustrate: A young man is interested in Journalism, but he has been wisely advised against majoring in it. Instead, he takes his Journalism course as his number one minor subject. He works on the school paper and he contributes to the campus humor magazine. But his major field of study during his undergraduate training is *History*. In addition to his major, he takes as many English courses as possible. When he graduates, he finds that Journalism is the career for him. With his broad background in basic studies, he is able to present himself to any managing editor as an *educated* man. The editor can teach him in a matter of weeks the technical requirements for reporters on that particular newspaper. The young man will not have had to spend hours of academic credit time learning what can be taught so readily on the job. And, in time, with his solid foundation, this broadly trained young man can become a top-flight newspaperman. He used his four years in college to prepare himself for *future growth*. What better use to make of it?

Over the past fifteen years, I have discussed this problem with several newspaper editors. In almost every case, the editors have told me quite directly that they would rather hire a Humanities major than a Journalism major. I can back this up with my own experience in the field of Broadcasting. When I have had the opportunity to choose, I have hired English majors instead of Radio-TV majors because I felt they were more likely to be solidly educated and more able to grasp ideas and create new ones.

Now, I realize generalizations are dangerous. So let me hasten to make the necessary reservations about these opinions I have stated in such general terms. There are, most certainly, many departments of Journalism, Speech, Drama, Radio-TV, etc., that turn out well-rounded, *educated* graduates who are prepared to excel in their chosen field of endeavor. But there are also many that do not.

Our primary concern in this discussion is with the young person who enters college without a clearly defined major field of interest. If you are one of those individuals, I urge you—in summary—to consider well the following points:

1. Do not feel insecure. Instead, accept the opportunity to get a broad-based liberal arts education at the undergraduate level. In the long run, it can prove the most valuable.

2. Do not take refuge in one of the "professional" majors just because you think every student must be able to say what he wants to be when he finishes school. Explore these specialized fields as minor courses and extracurricular activities.

3. Remember that at this moment in our history there is a world of opportunity for the individual who has trained himself to think, to learn, to build, to create, to work with ideas and concepts. If you keep your horizons broad, you put no limit on your future.

For more practical suggestions, next page . . . please . . .

THREE PRACTICAL
GRADE BOOSTERS

FOR ANYONE who intends to get the most out of his time in college, and to have a good record of grades to show for his efforts, I submit three practical suggestions. They are not revolutionary and I am sure you have heard others expound in great detail on the same three points. They are, however, so fundamental to an efficient use of your time in college that no discussion of this kind would be complete without them.

1. Make up your mind right now that you will keep class cuts down to an absolute minimum. There is no substitute for that hour spent at a lecture. You can read yourself dizzy in the library, you can ques-

tion classmates till you're blue in the face, you can memorize your text book, you can spend hours trying to make up the work . . . but unless you sit in on each of those class lectures, you're going to do it the *hard* way. This happens to be one of the facts of college life, and yet you find students on every campus who make a point of cutting as many classes as they can. It's foolish! That hour in class can mean more than four hours of study. It can, that is, if the hour is spent with the attention on what the lecturer is saying. (Again, the secret ingredient: *Concentration.*) If you will attend class regularly, *concentrating* on the flow of ideas as they are presented to you, you will find you need to spend fewer hours outside the class to master the subject and make the grades.

2. Learn to take lecture notes. Take them regularly and take them right. Put down the important points that you hear the lecturer stress—and write legibly. (No matter how good your intentions may be, you probably will not find time to "transcribe" notes later; and, anyway, why spend twice as much time as necessary?) Do not crowd your notes. Give the important points plenty of "White Space" so that they will stand out when you are reviewing your notes. If you miss a class or two during a semester, borrow somebody else's notes each time. When

exams roll around, you should have a complete, lecture-by-lecture picture of the course as it was presented, with the stressed points right there before you to remind you of the instructor's emphasis on them. (They're likely to be the exam questions!) Nothing will serve to jog your memory better and give you a more thorough understanding of what the instructor tried to convey to you than a COMPLETE set of notes in proper sequence. Good note-taking is *not* a lot of work; it's simply a businesslike *habit*. School libraries have material that will give you suggestions about good outline procedure. Look over some of the "systems" you find in these books, and then work out your own. There is only one rule for good note-taking: the notes must make sense when you are going back over them. Your own clean, neat, comprehensive set of lecture notes can make the difference of from ten to twenty points on any final exam score. You might as well have those points. So get the *habit*—take your notes regularly!

3. A typewriter is a college student's best friend. Shop around and pick up a sturdy secondhand standard machine or a portable that works well. If you have not learned to type in high school, make up your mind to spend two or three weeks learning to operate it. That's all it takes—a typewriter, some time, *concentration* and a touch-system chart. You'll be

surprised how soon you catch on to the technique; but . . . don't try to do it the "easy" way . . . with one finger! No matter what kind of course you take, upper-level education calls for expression of ideas. You will have to submit papers, papers and more papers. And unless you are the one person in eight thousand who takes pride in his penmanship, you will want those papers to be *typed*. If you have a small fortune, you *can* pay to have them done, but your expression and your spelling . . . and your *marks!* . . . will be better if you type your own work. (To say nothing of your bank balance.) No matter how intelligent you may be, no matter how great a student you are and how thoroughly you do your research, you must be able to present your ideas and/or findings in a neat, clean, sharp fashion. A messy paper has two strikes against it before the instructor starts grading it. So, neaten up and write right. For most of us, that means *type*-write.

Now, let's turn our attention away from the classroom and the books to look at another side of college life.

THE DOUBLE LIFE
AT COLLEGE

IN ANY seven-day week, there are one hundred and sixty-eight hours. Even in college, the days have only twenty-four hours. Analyze those hours and how they are used and you should begin to get a picture of an average student's major activities at college.

Start with the actual time spent in being exposed to instruction: classroom lectures, laboratories, field trips. With a normal course, about twenty hours a week are occupied with this activity.

The "rule of thumb" for study is "two hours for every hour of classroom lecture." (It's a solid rule, based on practical experience, and the student who tries to beat it, cheats only himself.) So, put down thirty hours a week for study.

(This is minimum!)

For muscles and mind and nervous system that work as hard as those belonging to the average college student, sleep is an absolute essential. Without it, something begins to wear out too soon; in some instances, it's the nervous system; in others, it's the muscles; and, unfortunately, sometimes the mind tires first. To keep the body together, SLEEP should be allotted at least fifty-six of those one hundred and sixty-eight hours each week.

Add them up: 20 hours for classes
30 hours for study
56 hours for sleep

Total: 106 hours

Leaving . . . sixty-two hours a week for the social side of college.

About one-third of your time is spent in some kind of social activity while you are in college. That's fine. It's all part of the experience of college. It's part of the experience of life. To be able to work and to play well with other people is part of the equipment you need for "the race." To pretend that the social side of a college life is something to be ignored is to shut your eyes to an essential aspect of the whole growth experience.

It is, by no means, the *only* aspect of college.

It is not even the most important aspect.

For no student should it be more important than the experience of the *solid* business of college: *academic accomplishment*.

But, also, no one should fool himself and think that it is *possible* to spend *all* of his time in college in pure academic pursuit.

The Social Side of College should be the fun side, the relaxed side, the balance that makes work more productive.

Like anything else, you enjoy it more if you understand it.

To understand it, look at it from every angle.

Let's talk about FRATERNITIES AND SORORITIES.

TO JOIN OR
NOT TO JOIN

THERE'S NO reason to paint a phony picture. The fact is that if you want to join and can't, either because you weren't invited or could not afford it, it's heartbreaking. There is a kind of resentful frustration that sets in, and it can make you mighty unhappy for a period of time.

It can make you unfair, too. It can make you think that everybody who belongs to a fraternity or a sorority is a snob. You can convince yourself that the Greek-lettered "elite" are bound together in a conspiracy to monopolize all the fun of college life. And you would be so wrong.

In the first place, just because someone got into a fraternity or a sorority does not make him a snob. A snob is someone who is so insecure within himself that he has to build himself up with a kind of personal inflationary system. A snob is a pathetic person. Pity him. And avoid him, *not* because you think he thinks he is better than you are. Avoid him, because a snob is dull . . . D . . . U . . . L . . . L. You'll have a better time, you'll get a lot more out of your time if you spend it with someone who lives with *real* values.

But don't make the mistake of branding *every*body who wears a Greek pin a snob. If you wanted a pin and couldn't get it, remember: there—but for the turn of fate—go you.

And that's the clue: it's a turn of fate. It's nothing that should keep a girl from dating a boy. It's nothing that should keep people with mutual interests apart, prevent their being friends. Nine times out of ten, after the first year in college, the chief difference between the "Greek" and the "Independent" is that they live in different houses.

So, for whatever reason you did not join a Greek letter organization, by all means do not keep a chip on your shoulder for people with pins to knock off.

In many ways, that turn of fate that kept you out of a fraternity or sorority during your freshman year did you a favor! Because, as the system now exists in most colleges and universities, there is much that is wrong with it. The general pattern followed by fraternities and sororities is this:

1. During the summer before the freshman year, the prospective member is "rushed" by relatives, friends, friends of friends, or casual acquaintances. Invita-

tions are sent out to "rush" parties during "rush week."

2. "Rush week" is the week before school registration. During that time, new students on the campus are entertained at the various sorority or fraternity houses and at the end of the week the big choice is made.

3. "Rushees" indicate their preference as to the organization they want to join and the organizations select the members they want. When the two get together, the "Rushee" becomes a "Pledge," and a period of getting better acquainted begins.

4. During the Pledge's first year in school, he or she is affiliated with a "house" and is subject to the controls and discipline his new social affiliation has set up for the embryo members. Through the year, there is "hazing": obligations, rituals, meetings with the members. Study halls and "big brother or sister" supervision help the new member through the academic rigors of the freshman year, and his social life revolves around the organization with which he has affiliated himself. In general, the freshman who has "pledged" a Greek letter organization enjoys a kind of protection that replaces, to a degree, the supervision he has known in high school. The

"club" replaces "the family," except he is now supervised by young people more nearly his own age.

In many real ways this system makes the first year a happier experience for those freshmen who commit themselves to it. But, like everything else, this "easier way" comes at a price.

With the concentrated socializing of rush week, neither the prospective new member nor the organization has a chance to evaluate in any intelligent fashion the actual compatibility involved. Superficial values are very apt to sway both of them. The result is that the wrong person may get with the wrong group, and too often they are both stuck with the arrangement. Unfortunately, the pressure is so great on the new member that, in his immaturity, he attempts to solve the problem by adjusting to the group; and this is not always to his advantage. As a matter of fact, sometimes it can have most unhappy results. In any case, it reduces his effectiveness as a student during that first year.

As for the "big brother or sister" supervision of the first year, there is much to be said against it. Any freshman who must have the help of a guiding hand to take him through his social life and to hold the watch on his academic accomplishment is a youngster who is not ready for college. Fraternities and sororities were not organized in the first place as "nursery schools" for immature freshmen. They are *social* clubs. They are designed to put compatible people together for the pleasure and benefit of social exchange. The freshman who just "gets through" his first year with that initiation and "pin" at the end of it as his primary goal is a poor, misguided young person who has been robbed of a whole year of his college education. That initiation and pin will do very little, if anything, to give him any real satisfaction in the years ahead. If there is any social advantage gained by having the "membership," it can be negated ten times by the loss of the fruits that could have been his if he had used his first year in college to set a firm foundation for future education.

This is not to say that *every* pledge loses out just because he spends his first year in the protective coating of a Greek letter society. It is to say, however, that it does happen sometimes and it should *never* happen.

Fraternities and sororities have a place on the college campus.

But . . . the current system should be modified to accommodate the original and valid intention of these organizations. A suggestion:

1. Prospective members should be rushed at the end of their freshman year. No student should be rushed who has not made better than a "C" average in his first semester. The pledging ceremonies should be held at the completion of the school year and no one should pledge who has not made a "C" average.

2. Instead of the "rush week" now held before school starts, that week should be devoted to the hazing and initiation rituals. Members of the fraternities or sororities should gather early each fall to initiate the new members they pledged the preceding spring.

3. No member should be allowed to live in a fraternity or sorority house until his junior year. Also, the school should maintain a strict rule that no student whose grade average falls below "C" may live in such a house.

Arguments for the system suggested above are obvious. The most important one is the fact that the calibre of fraternity and sorority members will improve noticeably if the groups take more time and use more effective measurements in their choice of new members. Pledging at the *end* of the freshman year will allow for that. (This, I realize, is the system now operating in some small Eastern colleges. It should spread to include state co-ed colleges.)

If these "clubs" are to continue with any vitality on the American campus, they must take steps immediately to improve their membership. Most often today, the leaders on the campus are "independents." Too often today, it is obvious that the good students on the campus do not have time for the juvenile high jinks that characterize too many Greek letter organizations. In the past twenty years, the prestige of these organizations has continued to diminish to the extent that now it is a rare campus on which they wield any significant influence. If they want to be "expensive fun-and-games" groups, good luck. Their future is a sickly one. The time has come for these groups to grow up and catch up with the increasing intellectual vigor that the nation's young people offer to the free people of the world as the hope for survival.

So, look well and wisely before you align yourself with a fraternity or sorority. If the group seems to be in the race as you must run it today, go ahead. Consider joining. But do not join until you *consider* it well.

If you feel a little shaky about your social adjustment and believe these groups could help you over a few social hurdles, forget it. You can make those hurdles by yourself.

Let's talk about those social graces. First, THE PHILOSOPHY OF MANNERS. . . .

THE PHILOSOPHY
OF MANNERS?

YES, there *is* a definite philosophy of manners, and it's something you'll have to know and understand thoroughly if you intend to "make good," socially. On the surface, good manners are simply a pattern of conduct. Just below the surface, good manners are a characteristic that makes you a pleasant person to have around, in any situation. And way down deep at the heart of the matter, good manners are a reflection of your attitude toward the people around you. That's where the *philosophy* of manners comes in, and to understand it completely, think about the way you got to be what you are.

Not so very long ago, you were a youngster, pretty much responsible to no one. Your parents taught you to say "excuse me" and "thank you" at appropriate times and to wait until somebody offered you a piece of candy before you made a pass at it, and so forth. They imposed a behavior code on you, which you followed to the best of your ability when older folks were around, and scrapped almost entirely when they weren't. This behavior code was rather meaningless to you as a child because *people* didn't mean much to you.

Eventually, however, you put aside your toys and started to become a social being. As you grew older, you grew more and more aware of the people around you. Almost overnight, many of them became important to you. Suddenly, what people of all ages *thought* about you MATTERED! Now, at last, something dawned on you: that code of behavior you followed mechanically as a youngster made *sense* and it had a very definite design about it. Doing the "right" thing made people more comfortable when you were with them, made them *like* you.

But at the same time, as you become aware of the importance of it all, it becomes a jumble of rules and regulations that are extremely confusing. These days, you wouldn't dash wildly down the sidewalk, bowling over all the little old ladies that happened to be in your path. You wouldn't take a sandwich out of your pocket and start eating it in church. Such things are obvious. But a lot of things *aren't* so obvious. All your life you've been walking in and out of rooms . . . and all of a sudden you feel like a fool when you walk into a room full of people. At the oddest times, you get a panicky sensation inside because you're afraid you'll do the wrong thing. You never know quite what to say and how to say it. Even your hands and feet become hard to manage. But!—somehow you can't escape the feeling that if you could master this *manners* business, you'd have the answer to about ninety per cent of your troubles.

Well, you're *right*.

Start by looking for the why's behind each rule.

Check over some of them:

Men extend various courtesies to women and girls because by nature males are helpers and protectors of females. "Ladies before gentlemen" is one of these courtesies, and the reasons for it are quite understandable. It's a rule that holds until there's a *hazard* involved. Then, the man goes first. For example, a man gets off the bus first to help the lady down, because he doesn't want her to stumble or fall. He opens doors for women because men are expected to be stronger than women. A man holds a woman's coat and her chair because he wants to *help* her with any social activity she finds difficult. Just as a man holds horses while she mounts and car doors while she gets in, he steadies canoes for her and performs countless services that are intended to smooth the way and make things easier for the lady. Sir Walter Raleigh was up to exactly the same tricks when he tossed his coat over the puddle!

Men are the helpers and protectors of womankind. They stand when a woman enters the room because it shows respect. They step aside when they are in her way, for the same reason. It all follows the same pattern.

Women, on the other hand, have an obligation to the men who have shown them respect, tendered them the courtesies that our way of life has made customs. A woman should give pleasure to the man who has been gracious enough to open a door, hold her chair, step back and allow her to enter first. It is her responsibility to make the person who has honored her pleased that he had so done. (Good manners are give-and-take.)

A woman's *voice* is a personal aspect, but it is very much a part of good manners and should be mentioned here. With her voice, a woman can offend the basic principles of manners. When a woman's voice is shrill, loud, it is unpleasant. When something that a person does makes someone else uncomfortable, then that person is guilty of bad manners. Ergo: a loud, shrill voice is bad manners. Although the rule applies to both men and women, it is something that women should watch more carefully. The loud, irritating voice of a woman can do more to destroy her appearance as a lady than almost anything else she can do. Both women and men should remember a single guide: Speak clearly so that you can be understood by the person or persons to whom you are addressing your remarks; be sure that no one *else* hears you.

In the matter of introductions, the rules are based on solid logic. Women are generally expected to remain seated when they are introduced to someone. *However,* when the person being introduced is a woman or a man who is older than the lady, she should show the elder person the respect due his age and rise to accept the introduction. Men always rise to be introduced to anyone, man or woman. As for the sequence of the names involved, there's a logical pattern. If you take Lucy home to meet your mother, you walk in and say, "Mother, may I present Lucy Jones?" You've said it that way because your mother is the older of the two and deserves the greater respect. You've *presented Lucy to her*. And, you'll notice, you mentioned the name of the one due the greater respect *first*.

You'll find complete instructions in the etiquette books in your library. When you read these books, the point to remember is that all rules of etiquette are based on logical patterns. There are definite why's behind each "good manners" practice. Look for the pattern, the *why* behind a situation, and you'll come up with the right thing to do every time. If you want basic principles to follow, try these:

1. In the company of others, a human being should be ever alert for the comfort, convenience and happiness of those about him. If he conducts himself accordingly, he'll replace social blunders with social triumphs.

2. A man should have a natural, deep-seated respect for all women. He should be willing and anxious to serve them and to please them at every opportunity. A lady should be gracious and grateful for a man's courtesies.

3. A social situation is always a give-and-take situation. You are socially adjusted when you learn to fit in with others and *contribute* something. Simply to "take" is not enough. You must bring to every social situation some quality that will make other people happier because you're there.

The philosophy of manners is, in reality, nothing more or less than the art of living comfortably, happily and successfully with other people.

You spend a lot of time *eating* with other people.

Let's be sure you do it pleasantly. . . .

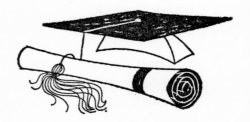

TABLE MANNERS

A GREAT many college students these days carry the table manners practiced while members of the lollypop set right through their teens, twenties and beyond! It's probably the result of embracing a notion that all manners are silly to begin with, and backing that up with the equally absurd notion that you perform fundamental chores like eating—simply by doing what comes naturally. If you've fallen victim to this sort of self-delusion, forget it. There's a bit more to eating than stuffing your face. A good set of table manners is: (1) easy to come by; (2) the simplest, most logical rules you'll ever run into; and (3) like money in the bank for the person who wants to move forward in "the race."

You spend some of the most important hours of your life eating. You'll find that many of the most important people in your life are those who are with you when you eat.

Table manners are simply rules that make the *mechanics of eating* a pleasant experience for the *other* people who are at the table with you!

Let me illustrate with one rule here, and then you can apply the idea to all the other rules that follow:

It is *not* acceptable to take a full slice of bread, spread it with butter, peanut butter and jelly, and then launch into the full slice, hacking off semi-circular portions as you go. You are supposed to break the bread into small bite-size pieces (or quarters), spread whatever you want on one section at a time and proceed to *eat* one section at a time. This same goes for rolls: break off and eat a bite at a time. It may be a little more trouble this way, but other folks at the table with you get a better view; you *look* better when you're not carving cookie cutter patterns with each bite.

Keep the idea of how you look in mind, also the idea that the comfort of others is *always* your concern—and the following basic table manners will make sense:

MEN:

Stand until everybody is ready to sit down at the table.

Hold the chair for the lady (or ladies, if you can get around to more than one, and there are not enough men). If you're the only man and there are several ladies, make the gesture for the hostess. Your mother, for instance!

WOMEN:

Acknowledge courtesy if it's extended. Allow the man to hold your chair, seat yourself easily and quickly, not causing him to stand there awkwardly, not knowing if you're going to sit down or not. If for some reason no man is immediately at hand to help you with your chair, go ahead and seat yourself. If the man forgets to do it, or if he is busy with someone else, your obligation is to let him feel no concern about it. It is *bad* manners ever to remind anyone else of the so-called *good* manners.

MEN & WOMEN:

Sit *relaxed*, but don't collapse all over the chair and table. Dining-room chairs usually have straight backs, *your* back should be the same.

Put your napkin in your lap as soon as you sit down. Arranging it later may hold up the serving.

Bring your food *up* to your mouth. Don't try to hook your lip on the edge of the plate and *slide* the food in! Heads that are constantly bobbing up and down at the table are most distracting. Make sure yours doesn't.

When you're eating soup, dip your spoon toward the *far* edge of the bowl or cup, and don't load it so you have to do a "steady-hand" demonstration.

It's permissible to tilt the bowl for that last spoonful, but tip it *away* from you.

If the soup bowl or cup has handles on it, pick it up and drink the soup after you've tasted it with a spoon. Noodles, vegetables and so forth will be eaten with the spoon.

You don't have to drop your silverware after each "stroke," but don't brandish it about, to punctuate your conversation.

Even your *plate* should be kept shipshape at all times. Don't overload it. The cook is flattered when you accept seconds. Don't *ask* for seconds, however, until they're offered. They will be, if there's enough! If you want to refuse a second helping, just say, "No, thank you." No discourse on how *full* you are! Or the fact that you are on a diet!

Cut and eat one piece of meat at a time. After cutting, some people eat meat with the fork still held in the left hand. It's the continental method . . . and it's becoming more and more popular in this country. But if you've always transferred the fork to your right hand after the cutting chore, continue to do so. Remember to be graceful and at ease at all times; there's no point in learning a new technique when the one you're accustomed to is perfectly correct.

You are supposed to be able to eat your salad with just your salad fork. Some rule books say you should *never* cut it with a knife, but if you can't rip off a section *without* your knife, go ahead and use it. Like everything else, you work on one bite-size unit at a time.

When you have finished eating, put your silver on the plate in such a way that it can be picked up easily, or the plate can be picked up with the silver on it. This means the silver goes across the plate. The custom is to keep the handles to the right, but that's an unimportant detail. Just remember that you're trying to *avoid* having silver slip to the tablecloth or the floor. That's what probably will happen when you put the tip of the knife on the edge of your plate and the handle on the table.

Try not to let your used silver slide into the food that's left on your plate. Always keep the handles of the silver clean.

To take something *out* of your mouth, simply reverse the procedure you followed when you put it in. If you put it in with a spoon, take it out with your spoon; if you put it in with your fingers, take it out with your fingers, and so on. But, try to avoid the need for taking things out of your mouth. Cut away fat and gristle from meat. Try to get the pits out of fruit before you put it in your mouth. If you run into a fishbone, a piece of basting string, or shot, remove it with your fingers as quietly as possible, and be on the alert for such hazards through the remainder of the course.

Never refuse food because you simply don't *like* it. Take a little. It won't hurt *you* and it *would* hurt the feelings of your hostess to know she had prepared something you didn't like.

If a certain food actually makes you ill, refuse it in the least noticeable manner possible. Or, take a small portion and just leave it on your plate.

To refuse drink (such as wine or liquor) use the same basic rule: consideration of others. Just say, "No, thank you," and don't make a big thing of it. Never turn a glass over or imply in any way that you don't *approve* of the liquid being offered.

Do *not* take food directly from the serving plate and put in into your mouth. When small sandwiches are served at a party, take your cue from the presence of small individual plates. If there are plates, put your food on one of them before you start to eat. If no plates are in evidence, then your sandwiches are being served as hors d'oeuvres, and you may eat them directly. At dinner, when olives, pickles, etc., are served, put them on your salad, bread-and-butter or dinner plate before you start to eat them.

Do *not* take sugar with the coffee spoon you are using.

Do *not* take more food on a spoon or fork than you're prepared to eat with one bite.

Do *not* mop up gravy with your bread, unless your hostess tells you it's OK to do so.

Do *not* act like you're starving to death. Enjoy your food, but remember the other people at the table and be sure there is food left for someone else.

Do *not* mix your food together in the middle of your plate. If meat, potato and vegetables wind up on one and the same plate, keep them in different parts of the plate.

Do *not* risk getting the edge of a drinking glass greasy. If necessary, wipe your mouth clean with your napkin before you drink.

Do *not* push your plate away when you finish eating.

Do *not* light up a cigarette when you're through, unless ash trays are provided on the table, and the hostess invites you to smoke. It's always better to let someone else start to smoke first.

Do *not* lean back in your chair or try to cross your legs under the table.

And do *not,* whatever you do, forget to say you enjoyed your meal—even if you didn't! If you've been considerate of others, if you've tried your best to look your best while eating, and if you've appeared to enjoy your dinner . . . your hostess will be mighty glad you were there.

Regarding the use of silver . . . because of the age-old "which fork" gags, you may have an idea it's really *difficult* to figure out which is the proper implement to use on what food at what time, during a full-dress dinner.

It's not the problem you might expect, but don't be upset if you really are or have been befuddled by that gleaming array of knives, forks and spoons. You may not be accustomed to using a full set of silver in day-today eating in your home, and it's only natural to experience some confusion. The truth is, however, the problem is easily solved.

Each piece of silverware is designed to function best in a particular job. To illustrate, a *soup spoon* differs from a *teaspoon* in that it has a rounded and slightly deeper bowl. It would be rather unwieldy for stirring coffee, but it works out fine for eating soup. A *salad fork* has shorter tines (or "prongs") than other forks. Often the tine on the left-hand side of your salad fork is broader than others; this broad tine serves as a knife, since you are supposed to cut portions of your salad with it. With a steak or other meat that's hard to cut, you'll have a special knife for the purpose. Steak knives have either very sharp blades or blades with tiny saw teeth in them. Obviously, they are designed only to cut meat, not to spread butter on your bread. If you find duplicate pieces—identical forks, for example—they are intended to be used in two separate courses.

As for the proper way to *use* silver . . . if your table has been properly set, the silverware will be lined up in the order in which you will use it, next to the hand you'll use it with. Since spoons and knives are always used with the right hand, you will find them at the right-hand side of your plate. Forks are used, at least some of the time (while cutting meat, for instance) with the left hand. So, you will find them at the left-hand side of your plate.

A fundamental point to remember: it is far more important to appear at ease and act as if you know exactly what you're doing than it is to be doing the correct thing. If you find you are using a fork or knife that no one else at the table is using, either change quietly, or go right on using it. If you act at all flustered, your hostess will have failed, because your comfort, convenience and ease are her primary concern. Very often, a smart hostess who thinks she is entertaining one or two guests who are unfamiliar with some of the silver will cue her guests by being the first to use each implement. If you can't take your cue from her, check on some of the other guests. Usually, a little patience will pay off.

One more thing to keep in mind always: use the silverware lined up by your plate *only for eating*. You don't take sugar with your own spoon, or slice butter with your own knife, or spear bread or meat with your own fork. There will be a serving implement with almost everything. If there isn't then you are expected to use your fingers. (On the bread, for example, or the raw carrots and celery.)

Finally, and above all: you are to be a gracious dinner guest. If you are uncomfortable, your hostess will notice, and be uncomfortable herself. Relax. Choose the silverware you think will work best for each job, and if you are wrong, do not concern yourself or anyone else with so slight an error.

Now, from the dining table let's move our sights to the larger SOCIAL CIRCLE. . . .

THE SOCIAL CIRCLE

IN YOUR day-to-day, night-to-night relationship with members of the opposite sex, you will encounter situations that are neither critical nor complicated. Yet they can prove troublesome if you do not know readily what is expected of you. This is by no means a definitive discussion on social customs or etiquette. As I said a few pages back, there are big, good books on that subject, and I recommend you have a nodding acquaintance with those books in order to refer to them whenever you need a complete, authoritative answer. (There is no reason on earth why a man should find an etiquette book uncomfortable reading. Oddly enough, men are as troubled with the "proper" or the "accepted" manner of doing things as are women. And to know what is "accepted" is only to be more comfortable in the social activities that involve everyone.)

Since, however, we are concerned on these pages with your easy progress in the steady march forward through college, let's examine briefly some of the common problems which face both men and women in the social circle of college.

With the general philosophy of manners and the specifics of table manners behind us, let's consider now the social circle of *Dates*. No man or woman in college should be without them. With no intention of down-grading the romantic aspects, I suggest there are a few simple ground rules that are worth our attention. It's well to understand them and to appreciate them. It's very likely that you already know them. In any case, it will do no harm to check them over. They're mostly simple precepts that you first became aware of when you started dating. They're just as valuable to bear in mind in college as they were in high school. Specifically—

FOR THE *woman* ON *dates:*

To be consistent, the man is expected to ask the woman for the date. (In *normal* circumstances.) He is to be the host, so the right to extend the invitation is his. Since the woman is the guest, the right to accept or to refuse the invitation is hers. To accept, she need only say that she is pleased and then make sure that she understands the occasion and all of the essential conditions of the date. (When, where, what and how to dress.) To refuse, she need only remember that she is turning down an invitation and her responsibility to decent manners is to be gracious. She need not go into an elaborate explanation of her reasons for turning it down. She need not carry on about the extent of her regret. If she is to stall, she should have very good reasons for stalling. To be waiting for someone else to ask for a date is *not* a good reason. If there are circumstances that she must clarify before she is free to accept or forced to decline she should state clearly and concisely the terms of her delay. (Explain that you cannot give an answer at that precise moment. Then, go on quickly to tell your "host" when you will be able to give an answer. No need to go into the details. If he is willing to wait for the delayed answer, he has the next move.)

When the situation is such that the woman is in the position of extending the invitation (Sorority, club dances or parties are a good example), then she is obliged to abide by the rules that apply to any hostess. She should be reasonably sure that the man she is inviting is someone who will enjoy the occasion; it is always preferable for a woman to invite a man who has previously asked her out on a date. (This is no way to *start* a relationship!) The invitation should be extended clearly and specifically; *clearly* pointing out the occasion, when it is, what it is; *specifically* outlining the arrangements that have been made and what involvements the man will find himself in if he accepts. (Do not be so subtle and/or timid that the man is left confused as to the exact nature of the invitation. And, above all, be sure that your invitation is extended in such a way that the man may comfortably refuse it. Do not pressure in any way. Do not cajole. It would be much better to stay home than to go out with a man who took you against his will. If he refuses, receive his reply graciously, with no hurt feelings. He is probably truly busy and *unable* to accept. Remember: no man likes to feel like a heel. If you ever want to see him again, avoid a barrier that will keep him away in the future.)

When the man comes to pick the lady up, she should be ready. This applies to *all* dates, whether arranged by the man or the woman. It is *not* smart to keep a man waiting. A man who arrives for his date, only to find that he must wait while she dresses can draw two conclusions: (a) she didn't care enough about the date to prepare for it, or (b) she is a featherhead who cannot manage her simple affairs.

A woman should never put a man in a situation that will *force* him to spend money. On a date, *he* is the host. *She* is the guest. He must be allowed to make all suggestions that involve his pocketbook. (On the other hand, if—as a good host—he asks your preference, tell him— Which movie would you prefer? What do you want to eat on the menu? Do you want to go home?)

Even if a woman is having a terrible time, even if she would rather be any place else on earth—so long as the man is behaving like a gentleman and *trying* to entertain her, she should be a good guest. (Make every effort to let him know that his efforts are appreciated. In the long run, it does *not* matter that you have to spend an evening with a bore; it *does* matter if you turn out to be a bad sport and act like a spoiled child and reveal yourself as being essentially bad mannered.)

A lady should give the man time to be a gentleman. (Wait for him to open the car door. Step back so he can hold the chair for you. Allow him to give your order to the waiter. You tell him what you want to eat. He tells the waiter. Let him hold your coat.)

A smart woman never asks a man to take care of her personal belongings. No man enjoys carrying a woman's purse or comb or vanity. It makes a bulge in his pockets, and it is the woman's responsibility.

A lovely lady must—if she wants to preserve the illusion . . . use private facilities to repair her make-up, fix her hair, adjust her clothes. To perform these neces-

sarily personal operations in public is bad manners
and bad judgment. (Why should a man be aware of the
devices you use to look your best? He should only be
impressed with the end result.)

When a woman accepts a date with a man, she has
committed herself to spend the time on that date with
him. To spend it with others—either men or women—
to the neglect of her date is a serious breach of good
manners. (It represents the most callous kind of disregard for the feelings of another person and for your
own commitments.)

FOR THE *man* ON *dates:*

To ask a woman for a date is to extend an invitation.
It should be a simple, direct question that can be answered with a simple, direct reply. In his request for
a date, a man should specify when, what and how long.
(Do NOT put the woman in a position of explaining
what she is planning to do on a given night. Never ask
a woman what she is doing on Saturday night. It's none
of your business. If you want a date for Saturday night,
ask for a date, not a run-down on her plans.)

Once a woman agrees to go out with a man, he should
plan his time with her just as he would if he were
hosting a larger party. (Know where you are going,
how much it will cost, what you will do afterward, how

the transportation will be arranged. Have the whole evening in your mind so that you will be in charge of the situation from the beginning to the end.) *A good date is a good host.*

As a general rule, it is always better if a gentleman picks up his date at her living quarters and returns her there at the end of the date. Only the most unusual circumstances justify a man's allowing a woman to meet him at a "mutually convenient place" or to return home alone. (If you have to make an extra effort to save her any inconvenience, that is part of your responsibility as a host. And—it will never fail to please a lady to note that you have inconvenienced yourself for her comfort. After all, to please that lady is behind everything you do on a date. Why else take her out?)

The smart man who wants to make a good impression on a date is always *aware* of her. He knows what makes her uncomfortable. (For instance, if she does not drink, he makes sure that she is never in the position of having to ask for a non-alcoholic drink; he takes care of that. In *all* situations, he is alert to those elements that might cause her discomfort.)

FOR *men* AND *women* ON *dates:*
Good Taste" is the key to a successful date. If you would be a desirable partner for another person's pleas-

123

ure, conduct yourself within the bounds of good taste and you are far on the way to achieving your goal.

But what *is* "GOOD TASTE"?

That's a question worth considering. Let's move on to it now. . . .

GOOD TASTE

IN "THE RACE" at every turn you will encounter an issue that is judged or evaluated on the basis of that illusive standard referred to as "good taste." For those who have it, it serves as a kind of personal radar, keeping them in the more acceptable channels of behavior and guiding their choice of material objects—their dealings with other people, their dress, their way of life avoid the offense known as "bad taste."

The mystifying thing about "good taste" is that you can't *see* it. You can never tell if a person is one of "good taste" simply by looking at him. And yet, most often the term is used to refer to material objects, to the surface gloss of a person. But the exterior can be deceiving.

To illustrate: Here is a girl who likes red. She will wear a red dress, a red hat, carry a red purse with red and white polka-dot gloves. (That sounds pretty bad, I admit; but this is an illustration.) As a person, this girl conducts herself in an easy, generous manner that makes everyone who comes into contact with her feel better. She is kind; she is pleasant, thoughtful, and never has been known to disregard callously the feelings of another person. Her speech is pleasant and graceful to hear. Her whole life is so oriented that other people blossom in her presence.

On the other hand, here are some people who find her choice of clothes distasteful. They are dressed immaculately —and quietly. Their homes are impeccable. They speak with great elegance about their choice of books, plays and art. In their dealings with others, these same people will discuss freely the cost of the objects they possess. They are rude to people who serve them. They are malicious and crude with each other. They get drunk. They display affections and passions openly. They are loud and annoying to others in public.

Obviously these people are guilty of the worst kind of taste. They display flagrantly bad taste in their *behavior;* and, yet, in their dress, in their surface gloss, they are the essence of good taste.

On the other hand, the girl who likes red displays the most obvious kind of bad taste in her dress; and, yet, her behavior is in impeccable taste at all times.

I submit that, fundamentally, the people described in the

illustration above have bad taste and the girl has good taste. Just as certainly as your eyes are on this page, what a person *buys* is only the superficial manifestation of his taste. The way a person *behaves* is the true test of taste.

The superficial manifestations can be learned very easily. The fundamental aspects of good taste have to be bred into a person, must be a philosophy that guides his whole way of life.

To take "the girl" of our story a step further. Assume that she is alert enough to recognize the difference between her dress and that of the other people who have mastered the "surface gloss" good taste. As soon as she becomes aware of the difference and begins to prefer the way the others look to the way she looks, she changes—it's as simple as that!

To emulate the dress of others who have been more successful in developing the "knack" of dressing with taste and effectiveness, all you need is a careful eye. Learn to appreciate the *under*statement in dress. Avoid the obvious or the glaring. Watch the grooming and the fit of your clothes. Check the small details.

The reasoning behind this need for "good taste" in the matter of dress is easy to understand. We humans are like other animals; as a protective device, we choose to take on the coloring of our environment. We simply are more comfortable when our *appearance* does not set us too far apart from our friends and associates. And—what is even more important in this consideration of our success in dealing with other people—our friends and associates are more comfortable with us if our appearance seems to fit in with our surroundings.

But, please note: I am NOT recommending here that you adopt such an attitude of conformity that you lose your individuality or your distinction. The point of this discussion about clothes and the superficial aspect of "good taste" is simply to stress the fact that it is wise to avoid the "gaudy" or the "too-noticeable" in your dress for the very sound reason that both you and the people with whom you are dealing will be more comfortable.

In the long race, however, the way you LOOK is *not* the determining factor in the success of your dealings with other people. The thing that really matters when it gets right down to the issue of a person's accomplishment is his attitude toward the *fundamental* aspect of good taste . . . his behavior; his desire to live close to the truth, avoiding the phony; his *attitude* toward basic values that motivate a decent, constructive way of life.

As you move forward through the years . . . in college, after college, etc. . . . . you will come to depend more and more upon this personal kind of radar we call "good taste." If progress is your goal, you must have a clear, uncluttered attitude toward it, *understanding* what it is, why it is important.

. . . Which gets us back to a point we discussed in our *word before* . . .

. . . Now, to a word *after* . . .

A WORD AFTER

YOU HAVE the picture.

In the steady march forward, the mountains diminish as you move near them and you find yourself on top after a climb. It's a gradual climb and the path is not so bad if you can keep your vision clear, accepting the guiding hands when they're extended and finding the stepping stones along the way. Trouble comes when the vision gets clouded by a mixed-up attitude. That's what we've been talking about.

As I said before, I hope your path will be a little clearer and your progress steadier after these discussions.

Now, also as I said before, the second section of this book deals with *facts* . . . facts that often are hard to come by in books written for young people who are about to enter into the experience of life on a college campus.

There are many terms, places, people, institutions that confront an individual when he starts to investigate the way of life at college. Many of them are new and he has never had an opportunity to deal with them before. So, as a help for anyone who is either loking forward to college or who is now involved in getting acquainted with college life, I have arranged these short, factual descriptions of pertinent information in alphabetical order, according to the subject.

For a lack of a better word, we call it a GLOSSARY.

Any questions?

Please look ahead . . . in alphabetical order.

GLOSSARY

ADMINISTRATION

Term used to refer to the top officers or officials charged with administering the academic program and the organizational affairs of the college or university. Officials with whom you are most likely to have dealings are:

REGISTRAR (AND DEAN OF ADMISSIONS): Customarily attends to admission, registration, scholastic records, administrative publications, other publications, miscellaneous examinations, sometimes space assignments and schedules of classes, refunds of fees, supervision of scholarship programs, diplomas.

COMPTROLLER (sometimes called BUSINESS MANAGER, BUSINESS DIRECTOR, FINANCIAL OFFICER): The business manager of the institution, the representative of the President in the supervision of all strictly business operations of the college or university not specifically assigned to some other officer. Duties include management of institution's lands and their appurtenances (leasing, surveying, buying and selling of products therefrom), rentals and upkeep of property, investments, trust and endowment funds, supervision of securities, purchasing of supplies and materials, supervision and maintenance of buildings and grounds, inventory and custody of property, general supervision of dormitories and eating facilities, construction.

AUDITOR (usually under Comptroller's general supervision): In charge of the accounting and auditing for the institution. Duties include bookkeeping, issuing and checking of requisitions, vouchers, etc., to see that they are properly charged and covered by funds, checking of expense accounts, depositing of funds, signing of checks, recording receipts and disbursements, keeping financial records.

BURSAR (usually under Auditor's general supervision): Paymaster, purser, or disbursing officer of the institution, responsible for salary records and payments to faculty, staff and student employees, for withholding of tax, medical, or retirement funds.

ADVANCED STANDING

This classification enables you to take a course at a higher academic level than the course which is normally required, if you have the equivalent of the course content either in knowledge or training. Your eligibility for such special status is determined by ADVANCED STANDING EXAMINATIONS, which are designed to assess your level of knowledge, understanding, achievement and ability. Advanced standing examinations are often given to incoming freshmen to indicate proper placement in certain courses or sections of courses. They generally are available also to graduate students, to expedite performance of graduate work.

ATHLETIC COUNCIL

Intercollegiate Athletic Council typically composed of representatives from Students' Association, Ex-Students' Association and faculty of the college or university, and is charged by the Administration and General Faculty with responsibility for and jurisdiction over all athletic games, meets, exhibitions, or contests with other colleges or outside organizations, and with co-ordinating these with intramural sports, required physical and health education and general physical welfare.

BLANKET TAX

Sometimes called ACTIVITIES TAX, GENERAL TAX, STU-DENT SERVICES TAX. Compulsory on many campuses, optional on others. Receipts from the tax are used to support worth-while campus organizations, services, activities on a pro-rated basis. Payment of this charge (amount varies from school to school) usually entitles you to identification card which will admit you to most major athletic events, cultural events, campus entertainment events (at no charge or at greatly reduced charge), and will enable you to receive the college paper, the handbook covering activities, or other special considerations.

CAMPUS BOOKSTORE (OR BOOKSHOP)

A very limited term for a very "unlimited" place. Your campus bookstore does sell books, new and used. (By used, we mean not only "second hand" but "third hand" and "fourth hand.") But this is only one small part of its function, which adds up almost to being "all things to all people." It will also offer you a vast variety of school supplies, records, drugs, cosmetics, household items, jewelry (purely decorative plus class and fraternity specimens), gifts, clocks, wastebaskets, banners, stickers, raincoats, T-shirts, stuffed animals, wares for decorating dormitory rooms (sometimes even curtains, rugs, bedspreads), stationery, greeting cards, bulletin boards.

The list could go on and on, or it may need to be shortened for some campuses. Whatever you want or need, it's a good idea to look first at the campus bookstore.

You'll find study aids there, too. Maps, globes, atlases, course outlines, study guides, paperback editions of required reading selections.

And when you're through with a course, if you don't want to keep your text—or texts—the campus bookstore will give you money for it. Not as much as you paid, of course, but some.

CATALOGUE

The publication or series of publications setting forth the rules and regulations of the college or university, and information concerning all facets of campus organization and activity, academic and otherwise.

In a large and complex institution, the CATALOGUE may consist of a number of volumes or bulletins, perhaps a GENERAL INFORMATION CATALOGUE concerning the college or university at large, plus DIVISIONAL CATALOGUES for specific divisions, such as schools, colleges, departments, agencies, or organizations. There may also be an ACTIVITIES HANDBOOK.

Publication is usually a responsibility of the Office of the Registar or similar official.

YOUR COLLEGE OR UNIVERSITY CATALOGUE IS YOUR FOUNTAIN OF KNOWLEDGE ABOUT YOUR INSTITUTION. GIVE IT THOROUGH AND CAREFUL STUDY.

Catalogue from any institution usually available upon request, with or without charge (which is nominal).

CHAIR

A teaching position (usually carrying special honor or distinction) for which the salary is paid in whole or in part by donations from an individual or group or organization not directly connected with the university or college. Donation may be given as a memorial. The term is used also to refer to the office of the professor who occupies the position. Examples: The Wesley Bible Chair, the Don C. Grimes Chair of History.

Used on some campuses to refer to any professorial post or specific professor's office.

CLASSIFICATION OF STUDENTS

Classifications designated FRESHMAN, SOPHOMORE, JUN-
IOR, SENIOR are NOT NECESSARILY synonymous with classifi-
cations designated FIRST-YEAR STUDENT, SECOND-YEAR STU-
DENT, THIRD-YEAR STUDENT, FOURTH-YEAR STUDENT.

Sometimes "first-year" and other designations by year
refer only to LENGTH OF RESIDENCE OR ENROLLMENT ON
CAMPUS.

FRESHMAN, SOPHOMORE, JUNIOR, SENIOR STANDING DE-
TERMINED BY NUMBER OF SEMESTER HOURS FOR WHICH
STUDENT HAS CREDIT, with classification determined by the
college or university and the requirements for the particular
degree.

(Examples: FIRST-YEAR STUDENT on SOME campuses is
student who has resided less than two semesters at the college or university. You might be a transfer from some other
institution, with JUNIOR STANDING but only ONE SEMESTER'S
RESIDENCE, THUS A FIRST-YEAR STUDENT.)

UPPERCLASSMEN—USUALLY refers to all students IN
ADVANCE OF FRESHMAN STANDING, but MAY mean ONLY
JUNIORS AND SENIORS.

UNDERGRADUATE—Refers to you if you have not yet received a bachelor's degree.

GRADUATE STUDENT—Means that you have one degree
but are working toward another.

COLLEGE BOARD

College Entrance Examination Board (administered by

the Educational Testing Service, Princeton, New Jersey). The Board's Scholastic Aptitude Test accepted in place of many specific institutions' Admission or Entrance Exams, if results satisfactory. Given several times each year, in all of the states of the United States and in established centers abroad. Fee for the Scholastic Aptitude Test is seven dollars. A booklet of information and sample questions may be obtained from College Entrance Examination Board, Post Office Box 592, Princeton, New Jersey. Dates are prescribed for testing and for application deadlines. Applications received after deadlines subject to a penalty fee of three dollars.

COLLUSION

Working with another person in the preparation of notes, themes, reports, or other written work offered for credit. Distinguished from COLLABORATION by your failure to reveal to the instructor the fact or extent of this co-operative effort.

COMMONS

Now a dining hall or common table shared by an organization's members or by special groups of students or faculty. Usually refers to the central public eating facility on the campus, such as the cafeteria in the student union. Faculty commons, however, may refer to a special dining room reserved for the college or university's faculty and staff.

COURSE NUMBERS

All courses are designated by numbers, or by numbers with letters (capital and/or lower case), and these are not just plucked from the blue. Used to indicate course rank and credit value in semester hours, and the part of the course, the semester, or term in which it is offered. Explanation of course numbers in detail may be found in the catalogue of the college or university.

DEAD WEEK

Week just prior to exams, when faculty asked to forego tests, written reviews, written reports, to allow you time for extensive review on your own.

DEANS

Administrators or directors of colleges or schools within a university, charged with the execution of all regulations and routines affecting their specific divisions. Primary jurisdiction over students and faculty in their colleges and schools, responsibility for scholastic welfare of individual students, for helping, advising, commending, reproving and dismissing, in accordance with the scholastic regulations.

The Dean certifies to the compliance of individual students with the requirements for graduation, attends to honors, to delinquent student lists, to majors and minors, to course prerequisites, to the adding and dropping of courses, and to absences.

Also DEANS in charge of all-university offices, agencies,

or divisions, such as Dean of Admissions, Dean of Women, Dean of Men, Dean of Student Life, Dean of Extension, etc.

DEAN OF WOMEN

NOT Frankenstein's Bride or the Mothball Demon of Yesteryear. More like a well-dressed, carefully-groomed Delphic Oracle . . . plus a sense of humor and an abiding desire to help you help yourself to all the rich and varied resources of the campus. Potentially the "hostess with the mostest," who's far more interested in seeing that you have a good time than in giving you a bad time.

I say "potentially" because some of you freshmen will be tempted to emulate the short-sighted senior who boasted of having been four years on campus without ever HAVING TO SEE the Dean of Women. A misguided miss, since discipline is 'way down the list with a small "d." Major attention in this office goes to housing, counseling, information-giving, special requests, student activities. All things to all girl people.

Housing? Responsible administrative office for regulations regarding hours and basic standards for housing of women students, with a creative weather eye out for the things, little and big, that will provide the best educational and living environment possible for each student. Instrumental in seminars, training courses, conferences with housemothers and other resident personnel, aimed at making home *really* sweet home, with conflicts eased, tension-knots untied, talents used toward enhancing attractiveness and "electricity" in the life of the place where you live.

(Dean of Women on most campuses looks with favor on growing trend toward self-government in student residences, with Dean's office in advisory and training capacity.)

Counseling, information, special requests? She's all ears (enlightened and sympathetic ones) for problems at home that keep you too upset to study . . . dismaying money matters and job needs . . . that "gargoyle" of a roommate you're stuck with . . . the prof who disliked you on sight and won't listen to reason. Could be you've hit a social situation that baffles you, and you don't want the girls in your orbit to know you don't know. To the Dean's office . . . with all due speed! Same path for those tricky questions like . . . say . . . there's sickness or a death in the family and can you leave the campus for three days without getting cuts?

Special activities? You, wanting to get into something besides books, and not knowing what. The Dean, ready to explore with you the places where your potential can be most productively put. Result: a meaningful minimum of activities that won't decimate your grade points, instead of a hyper-thyroid hodgepodge that leaves you flunked and fatigued.

Sorority activities are usually based out of the Dean of Women's office, with the sorority governing council, Pan-hellenic, being advised by members of the Dean's staff. Advises also in co-curricular activities involving women students: student government, honorary groups, service organizations, social groups, Student Union.

Now . . . discipline . . . last and really least. Emphasis not on punishment but rather on constructive help toward improvement. Doesn't mean the bars are down, but the insights are up. One point: Deans don't "snow" easily.

Summing up. When in doubt, or need to find out . . . go see the Dean of Women. If the answer's not in her office, she'll likely know where it is. And you'll be glad you went.

DEFICIENCIES

Lack of certain units of study required for admission, either from high school or as a transfer from another institution of higher education. Deficiencies may be absolved in specific instances with specific procedures. These vary from school to school. Wise to inquire. (And—do not put it off. Later is often too late.)

DEGREE CARDS

Cards or other applications filed signifying your intention to complete work toward and to receive a specific degree. Usually carry list of work completed and courses contemplated, and must be filed at certain time for careful check by competent official, to make sure degree requirements have been, are being, or will have been fulfilled.

DISCIPLINE

Where this term is used academically, it refers to a specific branch of learning. Though the dictionary says the use of the word "disciplines" to indicate various compartments of study is archaic, you will find the term used frequently on college or university campuses.

What constitutes a particular discipline? Well, it's a "way of looking" which characteristically shapes the things to be seen. For instance, the geologist, the historian, the philosopher deal with the same world, but each has the specialized approach to the things in that world which is peculiar to his distinctive "discipline."

DISCIPLINARY PROBATION

Suspended approval, involving certain stipulations and requirements for a definite period, as a result of your having violated college or university rules and regulations regarding student behavior and procedure. These penalties may include confinement to the campus, loss of dating privileges, non-participation in extracurricular activities, required maintenance of a certain grade level, periodic conferences with Dean of Men, Dean of Women, or some other administrator. Fulfillment of stipulations and requirements for the specified period results in removal of the probation; failure to fulfill leads to suspension, dismissal, or further disciplinary action.

EXTRACURRICULAR ACTIVITIES—
CO-CURRICULAR ACTIVITIES

EXTRACURRICULAR activities are those student activities

which are outside the classroom and are not connected, or at least not entirely connected with your straight academic work, but do have the approval, encouragement and supervision of the college or university. These include athletic and nonatheletic events and activities, such as football, basketball, track, glee clubs, orchestras, dramatic presentations, student publications, dance groups, interscholastic league work, special honorary and representative positions, miscellaneous public performances, and similar pursuits.

Where the activities in question are related to your course of study or where they represent a project which is a joint effort of several academic fields, the term "CO-CURRICULAR" is sometimes preferred. (Examples would be a light opera production, involving students from music and drama, and offered as an official production of both departments; a power show, in which students from engineering and the various sciences take part; the campus radio or television station, which offers practical experience to broadcasting majors.) The difference in terms is a rather "philosophical" one, with some people preferring to reserve "EXTRACURRICULAR" for purely social activities, while designating as "CO-CURRICULAR" all those activities which can be considered to offer an element of learning.

FINANCIAL ASSISTANCE

See LOANS AND SCHOLARSHIPS and STUDENT EMPLOYMENT

FOUNDATION

An organization or agency established for a specific purpose or purposes, financed with funds provided by the original donors, perhaps supplemented with bequests, gifts, or grants from others wishing to support the foundation's program of activities. Such a foundation may, by terms of its establishment, engage in study, research, teaching, community service, or the financing of projects related to its objectives.

Examples are The Hogg Foundation for Mental Health, the Ford Foundation (which underwrites many worth-while projects in education), the Fehr Foundation (which supports research in business and industry).

If located on a campus, the foundation's activities are closely interrelated with the activities of the college or university with which it is affiliated, but its efforts are not restricted to the university community. The Hogg Foundation for Mental Health, for instance, co-operates with university faculty members in mental health projects, many times supplying all or part of the funds for such projects, but this Foundation is active also in other projects throughout the state and in some which are national in scope. Though it has the control of its own budget, it handles its funds through regular University financial channels.

FREE GRADE

Such as: a Free *A*. MEANS A GRADE NOT NEEDED TO BRING A LOWER GRADE UP TO ACCEPTABLE AVERAGE, in checking grade points for honors or degree eligibility. Suppose you need a B or 2-point OVER-ALL AVERAGE for honorary fraternity qualification, with a certain number of "Free A's" specified for a certain number of semester hours. It will take 2 of your 6 *A's* to bring your 2 *C's* up to the required *B* average, leaving only 4 of your 6 *A's* as "Free A's," to be counted in the "Free A" requirement.

FRESHMAN COUNCIL

Orientation and governing body composed of freshmen on the campus, designed to offer opportunities for meaningful campus activities, to develop leadership, to involve first-year students in the varied aspects of campus government.

Representative FRESHMAN COUNCIL administered and directed by STEERING COMMITTEE, in which freshmen gradually assume leadership. At beginning of year, Chairman and Co-Chairman of Freshman Council Steering Committee are upper classmen, appointed by President of Students' Association. These officers appoint in turn a number of upper classmen to work with them in directing the Council, and in designating special committees to study various aspects of campus life. (Example: Judiciary Committee to study functions of Judicial Branch of Students' Association, Honors Committee to study honor and scholarship groups and opportunities.) Soon each Freshman Committee elects own Chairman. These Chairmen, plus these upper-class advisers, sit on Steering Committee, planning and co-ordinating all activities for freshmen—freshman dances, etc. At end of first semester, freshmen elect own officers and take over administration of Freshman Council.

GRADE POINTS

These are units of measure sometimes used in determining scholastic averages. Where averages are computed in GRADE POINTS, no differentiation is made in the number of grade points earned for a straight grade, a plus, or a minus. Typical grade point count goes like this: An A grade (A, A+, A—) entitles you to 3 grade points per semester hour of the class. (See "Semester Hour.") B gives you 2 grade points per semester hour. C gives 1 grade point per semester hour. You get NO grade points for D's and F's. Thus, an A grade in a 3-hour course for one semester: 9 grade points.

Taking five 3-hour courses in one semester, you would earn credit for 15 semester hours toward the total required for your degree, PROVIDED YOUR GRADE POINT *Average* (from all five courses) DOES NOT FALL BELOW "C" or 1.

Suppose you made 1 A (9 points), 1 B (6 points), 2 C's (3 points EACH), and 1 D (0 points), your total would be 21 points. Dividing your 21 grade points by your 15 semester hours, you arrive at A SEMESTER HOUR-GRADE POINT AVERAGE for that semester of 1.4 grade points, or slightly above the required C average.

In many universities using the grade point system, a grade of D will let you pass the course and you will not need to repeat the work, but it adds nothing to your grade point total and therefore threatens your OVER-ALL MINIMUM

SEMESTER HOUR-GRADE POINT AVERAGE OF "C" or "1" WHICH IS REQUIRED FOR PROGRESS TOWARD YOUR DEGREE. In other words, to get a degree you must have at least 1 grade point for every semester hour taken.

GRADE SYMBOLS

Used under certain circumstances to report a student's standing in the semester's work, where regular grade has not yet been earned. Examples: P (if you have been permitted to postpone an examination) . . . R (if you have been permitted a reexamination) . . . X (if, under specific circumstances, you have incomplete class or laboratory work).

GREEK

Signifies member of a sorority or fraternity or used to designate anything referring to sororities and fraternities.

HONOR SOCIETIES

Oganizations with membership or eligibility for membership determined by scholastic achievement. May be national or confined to your own campus. May be restricted to membership of specific class level, specific sex, specific area of study. Membership may be automatic (upon fulfillment of stipulated scholastic requirements), volitional (on same basis), or invitational (from among those eligible scholastically). Other considerations are character, interest, participation in related activities.

HUMANITIES (THE)

In earlier days (and in the dictionary) described as "the branches of polite learning regarded as primarily conducive to culture, especially the ancient classics and belles-lettres." (This last refers to literature of aesthetic value as distinguished from instructional or informative literature. For instance, poetry, essays, drama, orations and the like.)

Nowadays expanded to include other disciplines or branches of learning which are concerned with man's awareness of himself as a human being and of his relationship with the rest of mankind.

Considerable disagreement, though, on just what these branches are. Opinions range from traditional grouping (see above) to a combination which leaves out only the natural sciences and mathematics. Some in-betweeners list: "Classics, English, Fine Arts, Journalism, Modern Foreign Languages, Philosophy, Religion, Speech, and Drama." Others also include all Social Sciences (See Social Sciences) or some aspects thereof.

MAIN THING FOR YOU TO KNOW is what this term means in general and that there *is* CONTROVERSY concerning its coverage.

INDEPENDENT

Student not affiliated with social fraternity or sorority. Sometimes hear term "Independent Independent" or "Declared Independent," to designate member of organized non-fraternity group.

INFORMATION CENTER

Scope and location vary from campus to campus. Usually general information about campus and campus activities, places, people, procedures concentrated in special place for easy access. Wise to inquire where this is. May be a desk, a booth, a whole floor, an entire building. May be based in Student Union, Registrar's Office, Dean of Student Life Office, or Library. You DON'T HAVE TO KNOW EVERYTHING if you KNOW WHERE YOU CAN FIND OUT.

INSTITUTE

A division or organization for study and research which cuts across departmental or disciplinary (academic) lines. Example: Institute of Marine Science, whose staff members carry out research in several sciences on functional processes in marine environments and teach courses in several different departments.

"Institute" may also refer to a workshop, or seminar, or meeting of teachers or other professional people, which is designed to improve professional skills, increase professional knowledge and generally enhance professional competence.

INTER-FRATERNITY COUNCIL

Advisory-governing organization to co-ordinate, guide and assist fraternities in their efforts and activities. Membership consists of representatives from various fraternal organizations on campus.

INTERNATIONAL OFFICE

Aids and advises foreign students on the campus and coordinates special campus or community programs concerning these students. Good place to inquire about private tutoring in foreign language.

INTRAMURAL ATHLETIC ACTIVITIES

Activities "within the walls." Hence, athletic or sports activities confined to your own campus, with competition among students enrolled in your own college or university.

INTERMURAL ATHLETIC ACTIVITIES

Activities "between the walls." These are athletic or sports events and competitions in which your school and OTHER SCHOOLS participate.

LIBRARIES

Notice the plural. Many colleges and universities have separate departmental and other special libraries in addition to the Main or Central Library. These libraries are very important to you, because they are considered to be the *heart* of your university. Don't let yourself be overwhelmed by size of the system, number of branches, number of books. There are fairly simple procedures for getting the books and other references you want and need. With very little difficulty, you can master these procedures and make the library resources work with you toward your education.

These facts may help:

MASTER CARD CATALOGUE (ALSO CALLED "GEN-ERAL CARD CATALOGUE," "MASTER INDEX," "CARD CATA-LOGUE," "MASTER CATALOGUE"). Master key to the contents of the whole library system of your college or university. Made up of DRAWERS OF CARDS which include every book in every branch or stack or special room. Located in Main Library. (In addition to this, each branch or special division has its own CARD CATALOGUE of its particular books.)

DIVIDED CARD CATALOGUE. Means that the giant master card catalogue has its two index systems set up separately. In one division you will find the AUTHOR-TITLE approach used in card headings . . . in the other the SUBJECT-TOPIC approach.

(Where Divided Card Catalogue not used, the same card file drawers will house information on books available, catalogued in both ways.)

INFORMATION DESK. Presided over by an experi-enced, professional librarian WHO IS THERE TO HELP YOU if . . .

You don't know how to use the card catalogue (and lots of people don't, right at first) . . .

You don't know how to use the indexes . . .

You have a reference problem of any kind.

Won't do your work for you, but glad to help you do it. Can save you vistas of time. Usually has printed ma-terial handy to help you utilize the libraries to best ad-vantage.

STACKS. Shelves of books. OPEN STACKS mean you can browse at will. CLOSED STACKS mean you must present a Call Slip for the book you want.

CALL SLIP. This is the card or slip you fill out describing the book you wish. You fill it in from the information given in the Card Catalogue (book number, title, author, your name, address, phone number) and present it at the Loan or Call Desk, sometimes called Circulation Desk.

LOAN DESK, CALL DESK, CIRCULATION DESK. Where you turn in books you are returning and request books you need.

INDEXES. Card Catalogues list and index BOOKS ONLY. Contents of periodicals, such as MAGAZINES, JOURNALS, DIGESTS, NEWSPAPERS, are organized and listed for you in PRINTED INDEXES. Complete articles, stories, or other references in these periodical publications are classified in the PRINTED INDEXES by subject matter and author. For references concerning current events, for example, look under your particular topic heading or writer's name in, say, the *Reader's Guide to Public Affairs.* Periodical references to subjects concerning education will be found in the *Education Index,* articles on the theater in the *Drama Index,* and so on. Some indexes cover whole fields of interest, others only the contents of a particular publication, such as the index for the *American Psychiatric Journal.*

READING ROOMS. Often house reference books relating to some special field. Examples: Humanities Reading

Room, Business and Social Science Reading Room. Not basic book collections, but rather reference tools.

RESERVE BOOKS (MAY BE A SPECIAL RESERVE READING ROOM, MAY BE RESERVE SHELVES IN MAIN LIBRARY, MAY BE RESERVE SHELVES IN DEPARTMENTAL LIBRARY). Books which have been placed "on reserve" for READING ROOM USE ONLY or LIMITED TIME WITHDRAWAL. Means these are reserved by faculty members teaching courses for special use of the students in those courses. Books are on their required reading list and must be kept available for students in those classes. Sometimes available for one hour, two hours, one day, three days, etc.

LOANS AND SCHOLARSHIPS

Higher education is a costly business, and you may need help in financing your college or university years. Sometimes you know in advance of admission that your funds are inadequate. In other instances, you discover this only after you are on campus and meeting unexpected expenses.

In either case, you may be interested in the loans and scholarships which are available at many institutions.

Information and assistance in regard to these forms of financial help are likely available in large colleges or universities through a special Office of Loans and Scholarships. Otherwise, probably through the Dean of Student Life, Dean of Men or Dean of Women, or sometimes through the Business Office or Office of the President.

SCHOLARSHIPS: Office in charge provides application

forms and dates for filing toward fall and spring awards. May also have available list of scholarships offered and special requirements for specific ones.

Applications usually judged on basis of academic abilities, recommendations and need for financial aid. Usually must be accompanied by your application for admission to the college or university and by complete transcript of your previous academic record.

Frequently possible for you to file A SINGLE GENERAL APPLICATION and BE CONSIDERED FOR ALL SCHOLARSHIPS AVAILABLE.

Information concerning specific awards available on request.

LOANS: Usually of two types—SHORT-TERM and LONG-RANGE. Funds made available by the institution itself or possibly through the institution by some outside individual, agency, or organization. SHORT-TERM immediate help generally available only to assist you in meeting emergency situations. Small amounts, not adequate for financing broad educational program, but only to meet pressing and current college expenses. LONG-RANGE help in larger amounts to finance major schooling costs. Many repayable with interest after graduation, with payment plan stipulated.

Long-range example: NATIONAL DEFENSE STUDENT LOAN FUND, provided by the university and the Federal Government. Primary qualification is financial need coupled with ability to perform college work. For this help you must be a full-time student making normal progress toward your final educational goal. Special consideration given to you if you are (a) a student with a superior academic background who expresses a desire to teach in public elementary or secondary schools, or (b) a student whose academic background indicates superior capacity or preparation in science, mathematics, engineering, or a modern foreign language. Maximum loan: $1,000 per year, but specific amount lent to you determined on basis of your need, the availability of funds, and evaluation of your scholastic ability.

Long-range assistance in larger and smaller amounts available from numerous other sources, differing from school to school, but sometimes available for you to use at a college of your choice (perhaps from a restricted list of possible institutions).

GRADUATE FELLOWSHIPS, ASSISTANTSHIPS, GRANTS: Vary from campus to campus. Inquiries should be directed to Graduate School (possibly the Director of Fellowships). Graduate LOANS probably handled through the office handling other student loans.

NATURAL SCIENCES

Include PHYSICAL SCIENCES (basic ones being Chemistry and Physics) and BIOLOGICAL SCIENCES (Bacteriology, Zoology, Botany, etc.). Biochemistry and Biology cut across departmental lines. Some aspects of Geography and Psychology are included in the Natural Sciences.

ORIENTATION

A special introductory program of activities designed to facilitate your entrance into your new campus community, to get you settled in your proper place (academically and otherwise), and to give you at least a nodding acquaintance with campus places and people, with regulations, procedures, activities, and services. Orientation is aimed chiefly at expediting the group processes necessary to make you a student in good and proper standing, while erasing the feeling that you are "a stranger in a strange land."

May be confined to the first few days of the regular school session, but many colleges and universities prefer to schedule the freshman orientation calendar prior to the beginning of regular classes. Special summer orientation sessions are offered on numerous campuses, often several during the summer. A summer session may last three or four days, during which you will eat and sleep in one of the dormitories, and you are usually eligible to attend if you have fulfilled your college entrance requirements and are planning to attend the regular college or university session in the fall.

The bulk of your time will be spent (morning, afternoon and night) in taking your required tests, attending convocations where campus administrators and student leaders will speak to you on special topics, seeing special orientation movies, loping about on conducted campus tours, asking questions in discussion sessions. This is the time to find out the things you want and need to learn from older students who know the ropes, and who are there to share their ex-

158

perience with you. It's also a fine opportunity to get acquainted with other newcomers, to begin building those human relationships which will add such vital coloring and substance to your life in college.

For information concerning orientation at the college of your choice, write to the Registrar, Dean of Admissions, Dean of Student Life, Dean of Men, or Dean of Women. Any one of these officials will be glad to help you.

PANHELLENIC COUNCIL

Advisory-governing council to seek co-operation among sororities, to unify the interests of sorority and non-sorority girls and to regulate rushing. Representatives elected from various sororities on campus.

PERMANENT RECORD CARD

The continuing and pemanent record of your work in the college or university, possibly including your high school transcript, admissions scores, test scores, courses taken and grades therein, honors received, work failed or not completed, sometimes major disciplinary actions, degrees granted, nature of your leaving. Material recorded will vary some from school to school, and your "card" may actually be a large sheet of regular paper or blueprint paper. Whatever its form, you should know where it is and be sure the facts are all there and accurate.

In most colleges or universities, your PERMANENT RECORD CARD is easily available to you for checking, if you can satisfactorily identify yourself. Often a duplicate of your permanent record is mailed to you at least once a year, with the urgent request that you examine it carefully to make certain that it is correct in every detail.

PERSONNEL SERVICES (*See* STUDENT SERVICES)

Include cultural programs, remedial services, vocational guidance, programs for physical fitness, out-patient and hospital services, psychiatric services and assistance with problems of personal and social adjustment.

Sometime called Student Services or Student Personnel Services.

PLAGIARISM

Academic larceny. Appropriation of passages, EITHER WORD FOR WORD OR IN SUBSTANCE, from the writings of another and the incorporation of these AS ONE'S OWN in written work offered for credit. May be (1) consciously embraced by unprincipled student who does not boggle at scholastic dishonesty, or (2) committed inadvertently by pudding-headed student who is hazy as to sources and/or untutored in the ethics of research. You're held responsible, either way. Research is an admirable pursuit, but GIVE CREDIT WHERE CREDIT IS DUE. More scholarly. Safer. And everybody (including yourself) thinks a lot more of you.

QUANTITY OF WORK RULE

Regulation of the college or university governing the

standard amount of credit work per week for an individual student working toward a particular degree. Maximum and minimum WORK LOADS (see WORK LOAD) are stipulated, with hour-grade point average required for quantity of work carried. Work loads permitted or required vary in quantity, depending on a number of factors, among them the length of the session, your classification as a student (see "Classification of Students"), scholastic ability, your age, your personal characteristics as a student, the nature of your courses, necessity for employment.

READING (REMEDIAL, CORRECTIVE, IMPROVED)

Your college may offer special classes, clinics, workshops, or tutoring for reading improvement. Slow or non-facile readers are wise to check with faculty member, Dean of Women, Dean of Men, or counseling and testing personnel about such services.

(To repeat a point made earlier: *Reading is the essential technique.* If you cannot read and comprehend what you read, it is very tough sledding, in or out of college.)

SCHOLASTIC PROBATION

Familiarly known as "Scho Pro." A period of suspended approval following substandard or unacceptable SCHOLASTIC performance. Your failure to achieve the minimum standard required for your classification at the end of a stipulated period (usually one long-session semester) puts you on scholastic probation for a subsequent stipulated period (usually the next long-session semester). If you fulfill scholastic probation requirements, you may be removed from probation. Failure to fulfill such requirements results in suspension or dismissal. Scho Pro stipulations cover minimum quantity of work, minimum grade levels, re-entrance, withdrawal, intercollege transfers.

SEMESTER HOUR

This is a measure of credit given for attending one class for one hour per week during a semester, which is eighteen weeks.

In a school which operates on the quarter plan, the measure of credit is a "quarter hour" which is given for attending one class for one hour per week during the quarter.

In general, the time spent in laboratories, field trips, studio activities, crew work, etc., is not counted for credit and will not affect the number of semester hours for which credit is given. Though frequently required as a bona fide part of the course in question, such work is considered supplementary to the regularly-scheduled classes which determine the semester hours earned for credit. Therefore, a course which has three regular classroom meetings each week during the semester will likely be a 3-hour course, although you may be required to spend six additional hours in lab.

SERVICE ORGANIZATIONS (*Student*)

Organized groups (generally honorary) with primary purpose of service—to one another, to the campus, to the community, to the nation. Some invitational, some open to all who meet requirements for eligibility (including scholarship, classification, character, participation, etc.). May be national or specific to campus. (Example: APO, national honorary organization, based on principles of Boy Scouting, extended to college men.) Good place to develop leadership, know campus leaders, learn about campus and community activities. Sample activities: ushering at campus or community events, guiding tours, officiating at elections and special procedures, such as registration, blood banks, ticket sales, fund collections, etc.

SOCIAL CALENDAR

Official list or docket of APPROVED and PROPERLY SCHEDULED social affairs or functions of students in the college or university. Frequently under jurisdiction of Student-Faculty Committee, jurisdiction applying to all student social affairs, formal or informal, and generally to all social affairs to which any student is invited. Regulations govern nature of event, approved guest list, dates, hours, chaperones, refreshments, etc. Length of time for registering event on Calendar in advance of date regulated. Social Calendar usually administered in office of Dean of Women, Dean of Men, Dean of Student Life.

SOCIAL SCIENCES

Those fields of scientific study which deal principally with man in his social relationships and his relation to his environment.

Here we generally find included Anthropology, Sociology, Economics, Government, History, the social aspects of Geography (such as the effect on man of his physical environment), and the social aspects of Psychology and Philosophy. Home Economics and Journalism sometimes included here.

SOCIAL PROBATION

Suspension of social rights and privileges. "Social Pro" invoked against GROUPS or INDIVIDUALS for infractions of university or college rules and regulations. Involves suspended approval for a stipulated period, with conditions governing procedure or behavior and restrictions in nature or amount of participation in campus activities. Fulfillment of requirements results in removal of the probation; failure to fulfill results in further disciplinary action, such as dismissal or the invoking of further penalties.

STUDENTS' ASSOCIATION

Sometimes called STUDENT COUNCIL, STUDENT GOVERNMENT, STUDENT GOVERNMENT ASSOCIATION, or the like.

Governmental organization of the student body for the general purposes of self-government. Customarily includes every bona fide student, as defined by the Registrar. By process of registration, you automatically become a member of the Students' Association, with a voice and a vote. Association usually operates within the framework of a Constitution and By-Laws, probably adopted by the student body and approved by the proper faculty committee or agency.

Representative Students' Association has EXECUTIVE, LEGISLATIVE, JUDICIAL BRANCHES, established and empowered by the Constitution, and operates through committees, considered a part of the Executive branch, and appointed by the President of the Students' Association. Organization as follows:

EXECUTIVE: President, Vice-President, Secretary— elected at large.

LEGISLATIVE: Student Assembly—some members elected at large, some from various schools and colleges within university.

JUDICIAL: Student Court—Chief Justice elected at large (from law students)—other members appointed by committee of campus honorary and legal organizations.

STUDENT ASSEMBLY

Legislative branch of student government. Sometimes called STUDENT LEGISLATURE, STUDENT SENATE, etc.

(See STUDENTS' ASSOCIATION—LEGISLATIVE BRANCH)

STUDENT COUNCIL

(See STUDENTS' ASSOCIATION)

STUDENT COURT

Judiciary body of Students' Association or Student Council.

(*See* STUDENTS' ASSOCIATION—JUDICIAL BRANCH)

STUDENT EMPLOYMENT

Many students earn a part of their expenses while attending a college or university.

WORK PROGRAMS are offered by some schools, whereby part-time employment on the campus, in dormitories, offices, laboratories, etc., entitles you to a stipulated portion of tuition or other expenses. These programs usually require certain academic standing for eligibility.

EMPLOYMENT FOR WAGES, part-time, on or off campus, usually on an hourly wage basis, is customarily permitted but subject to college or university restrictions pertaining to your maximum employment load and maximum academic load (with acceptable grades).

STUDENT EMPLOYMENT OF EITHER NATURE may be handled through a STUDENT EMPLOYMENT BUREAU, which also usually (1) aids and assists in finding vacation employment for students; (2) assists students, student wives and graduates in finding part-time or full-time positions; (3) provides counseling concerning vocational opportunities for college graduates and students; (4) maintains a collection of literature with up-to-date information on vocational training and preparation.

If there is no Bureau, may be handled through Dean of

Student Life, Dean of Men, Dean of Women, Director of Special Services, Business Manager, or (in small schools) sometimes through the Office of the President.

STUDENT GOVERNMENT
(*See* STUDENTS' ASSOCIATION)

STUDENT HEALTH CENTER

Varies in nature, physical plant and functions from campus to campus. May be only the office of THE college physician, for purposes of examination and referral, or the treatment of emergency, or minor, specific and acute difficulties (such as cuts, sprains, minor fractures and dislocations). May be small-scale hospital, clinic, or infirmary.

USUALLY, however, it is the FOCAL POINT FOR A COMPREHENSIVE HEALTH PROGRAM for your college or university, with responsibility for sanitation and public health regulations, the prevention and care of disease, the maintenance of the physical and mental health of the student body, the establishment and promotion of optimum physical student health conditions and environment.

Representative example is a state university which offers you these services if you are a regularly-enrolled student: (1) smallpox vaccination; (2) physical examination (including chest X-ray)—required for entrance to university and *processed* by Health Center if services performed by family physician, or *performed* by Health Center for you if you failed to secure services at home; (3) consultation and diagnosis; (4) emergency treatment; (5) hospitalization; (6) diagnostic pathological and X-ray examinations; (7) minor surgical operations; (8) eye, ear, nose, and throat examinations and treatment; (9) provision of an ambulance or automobile required to convey you to the Health Center from any point in the city; (10) accurate and detailed medical histories and records on you as a student.

Basic services are frequently covered by your Health Fee (which is usually compulsory), but certain special services carry additional charges. Usually you are NOT REQUIRED to consult a university physician, and you may be entitled to some benefits of the Health Center although under care of a private, non-university doctor. However, a university traditionally does not accept responsibility for you if you are not following advice and directions of official physicians, unless you are referred by them to a specialist, and it may not accept responsibility for you if you become ill when the institution is not officially in session. In this case, you may need to seek private treatment at your own expense.

Health Center is responsible for regulations pertaining to isolation and quarantine and for enforcing such regulations, and may require your withdrawal for physical or mental illness where such withdrawal is deemed in your best interest or that of the university.

Wise to be thoroughly familiar with rules, restrictions and facilities of your particular college or university. Learn these IN ADVANCE OF ILLNESS OR INJURY, in order that you may obtain your FULL BENEFITS under the special provisions of your own special institution.

STUDENT LIFE (Office of, Dean of)

Where this office exists on the campus, it is in general charge of all extracurricular activities for men and women.

Typical administrative line-up:

Dean of Student Life

Dean of Men

Dean of Women

Associate Dean of Student Life

Assistant Dean of Student Life

Its purpose: to supplement the academic program.

Its functions (may include):

Discipline

Housing

Information

Loans, Scholarships

Personal Help and Counseling

Records (Student Personnel)

Scholarship

Student Activities

Sometimes responsible also for:

Band

Intramural Sports

Union Activities (See Student Union)

International Students

Student Employment

Supervision of extracurricular activities for women is concentrated in office of the Dean of Women. (See detailed discussion, DEAN OF WOMEN.) The Dean of Student Life frequently supervises these activities for men, with the Dean of Men then in charge mainly of fraternity activities only.

Where the campus has no Dean of Student Life, offices of the Dean of Men and the Dean of Women are independent and self-directing, with Dean of Men supervising *all* extracurricular activities for men.

STUDENT PUBLICATIONS

Generally include yearbook, newspaper, humor magazine, literary quarterly, activities handbook and STUDENT DIRECTORY, any or all of these.

STUDENT SERVICES (*Office of, Dean of*)

Not on all campuses. Purpose of this office is the integration of all university organizations which perform functions predominantly of a student affairs nature.

Co-ordinates and generally supervises all student services (generally), including admissions, records and registration, student health, testing and guidance, intercollegiate athletics and student life, intramural athletics, and student union.

Main divisions at typical university are:

1. Office of Registrar and Director of Admissions
2. Student Life Office

3. Testing and Guidance Bureau
4. Student Health Center
5. Intercollegiate Athletics

Chiefly liaison between these offices and top university administration. Your contact as a student would be with the specific divisions.

STUDENT UNION (*May be called Student Center*)

Lounging . . . not labor. Generally considered the "living room" of the campus . . . the meeting place . . . the social center. On some campuses, the hub for *all* extracurricular activities . . . on others the focal point for just *some*.

Name comes from its dedication to unifying the diverse component parts of the campus . . . offering faculty, staff, students, parents and friends a place just to "get together" or to meet and concern themselves with the problems and development of the college or university.

Probably most versatile physical plant in your college sphere . . . with facilities for those who want to eat, greet, meet, or compete. Approximately seventy per cent have one or more kinds of food service, from snack bar to full meal. Usually big general lounge, plus specialty rooms. "Meet me at the Union" solves dilemmas of Dad-in-town-for-few-hours or love-life-stranded-while-I'm-in-class. Haven for ex-students who want to tap in again on favorite prof or make repairs between forays out to old haunts.

Meeting rooms allow all student organizations a place

171

to carry on their planning and organizational activities . . .
offer sanctuary for off-campus groups needing space to con-
vene or confer.

Want to dance? Bowl? Listen to music? Play your op-
ponent at ping pong or bridge? The Union is likely your
spot. Movies, too. Hometown papers. Radio. Television.
Parties, receptions, special dinners. Good place to start, if
you don't have other specific facilities in mind.

Home base for school spirit off the playing field.

Major meeting place of unorganized students on the
campus. Live in unorganized housing (private room, apartment, maybe sleep one place, eat another)? Not affiliated
with any specific group? Like people but not all-of-a-bunch-
like-bananas? Want to share some particular hobby or interest with students representing a variety of homes, social
and academic backgrounds? You'll find all sorts of com-
munion at the Union.

Swinging door to campus. Place to touch ground when
arriving . . . take off point for leaving. Probably offers
travel bureau facilities. Also may sponsor travel and study
tours. Frequently makes up car pools for rides homeward.

May be plain or plush. All levels, from small, limited
plant, for which students raised restricted funds . . .
through 4-million-dollar building with 200 hotel rooms
. . . to a 10-million-dollar Union complex resembling a
small town.

Ninety per cent of Student Unions supported by a compulsory fee, usually levied by the student body, with the students deciding the tax. Range: $2.00 to $20 per semester —national average $5.00.

Traditionally a laboratory for student citizenship. The Union is run by students to serve student needs; consequently its program is sensitive to student needs. Likely operates through a student council of some kind, with administrative officers and five to thirty-five or more committees: Committee on Ham Radio, for instance, or Art, or Games, or Charm, or Speakers, or Hi-Fi, or Publicity. Council operates with advice and direction of permanent, professional staff . . . some combination of Director (or Manager), Program Supervisor, Building Manager, Food and/or Games Director, Social Director. Faculty supervision varies. Sometimes several faculty advisers work with Council. There may be a Faculty Board or Committee concerned with general policy. (Rare instance: complete faculty supervision.)

Idea is to involve in Union activities as many students as can be efficiently used. Union committees are notoriously a good proving ground for campus citizenship and hatchery for campus-leaders-to-be. So if you're interested and want to work at something campus-oriented and constructive . . . don't hang back. You're wanted . . . very likely needed . . . and apt to be involved immediately, unless Union rules at your school preclude freshmen. (Some prefer newcomers to season a bit in freshman activities.)

To pinpoint procedure on your special campus, talk to any member of the professional Union staff or any member of the Student Union Council.

TEACHERS

Not a different breed just because they are called instructors, lecturers, professors, teaching fellows, etc. Your teachers are still concerned with helping you IF YOU ARE SINCERELY TRYING, INTERESTED IN GETTING HELP, AND WILL SO SIGNIFY. Main difference: you're on your own until YOU APPROACH THE TEACHER. By and large, college and university teachers have genuine regard for their subjects and their students, are pleased with and encouraged by SINCERE desire to learn on your part. If you're feeling lost and intimidated by the faculty-student gap, remember loneliness, inadequacy and isolation can be felt on the other side also. Teachers, too, need some "feed-back."

TESTING AND COUNSELING

TEST

test

Unpleasant word, most of us think, whether it looms large or small in our scheme of things.

And we've become accustomed during our early school years to thinking of tests as hurdles, obstacles, calculated to trip us up or slow us down in our usually pleasant scamper toward graduation.

Actually, testing has come to have a very different and

much more gratifying connotation in college and university thinking.

Now testing is seen as an integral part of the STREAMLIN-ING PROCESS in your progress toward your brand-new goal: a college degree.

Tests are used to facilitate your advancement, to remove obstacles to your speed and energy, to cut down the resistances that might impede your forward movement.

They are part of the extensive resources marshaled by today's colleges and universities to help you find your proper place, fit into it without undue stress and strain, with maximum effectiveness and enjoyment, so you can get on with the work ahead.

Admission tests and placement tests help to determine whether you are getting off in the proper race, in the proper place, in the proper starting position.

They serve to indicate on what level and with what group you will be most effectively accommodated in your study of English, foreign languages, perhaps science or mathematics.

Once past entrance or admissions exams, testing becomes a part of counseling, an important element in those rich resources for help and service which your college or university has provided for you. And this doesn't mean for you as an unusual person, or a lost soul, or an alien misfit. *No*, indeed. It means for you as a regular student, a representative newcomer to college life who shares the questions and confusions and hesitations and misapprehensions and anxieties that have plagued young people in this transitional period through many years.

You see, your role has changed. You are a freer, more independent agent than you've ever been before. The role and attitude of your teachers has changed, too. They have an interest in you, just as your high school teachers had, but it is a different kind of interest, which does not press itself upon you. The climate of your environment has changed. Expectations are higher than they have been in the past. Supervision is diluted. The atmosphere is far more impersonal.

Small wonder if you sometimes feel lost, baffled, frustrated. Or hanker for direction. Or hunger for advice and reassurance.

But you need not continue to feel that way. On most campuses, the help you need is provided in abundance, available from teachers, deans, administrative officers and counselors . . . available in all the counseling and guidance resources your school has placed convenient to your hand, ready to indicate changes in direction or to offer reassurance as to the direction you have chosen.

Frequently supplementing the routine services is a skilled staff in a Testing and Guidance or Testing and Counseling Center, trained to give expert assistance in academic, psychological, or personal problems. Testing is done by these people as a part of counseling, as a sharp and clinical instrument which can improve their service to you.

If the grade seems too steep for you, ability tests will help to assay whether you have enough horse power to climb the hill. Interest tests will help to indicate which hill.

Comfortable talks in a sympathetic but impersonal atmosphere may help you find that there was no steep grade, after all.

At any rate, you will have made an intelligent call upon the resources which can be fully effective only as students make their needs known. If you seem neglected, or feel neglected, it is likely that YOU HAVE NOT DONE YOUR FULL PART in seeking the assistance which it is highly probable your college or university has provided for you.

In all likelihood, the services available to you at your school are rich and varied. It behooves you to find out what and where they are. Hardly makes sense, does it, to flounder or just plain founder because nobody knew you needed help?

TESTING AND COUNSELING CENTER

Sometimes called TESTING AND GUIDANCE CENTER, PSYCHOLOGICAL SERVICES CENTER, or similar name. The office or offices responsible for providing psychological services to students and members of the university staff on campuses where these services are extensive and varied and organized in a comprehensive unit.

Supplements counseling given by teachers, deans and other members of staff. Generally responsible for administering tests required for admission, placement tests and various other testing programs. Assists teachers and departments with problems of measuring ability, interest, achievement. Probably maintains a staff of counselors to assist you if you need help with educational, vocational, or personal problems. Improvement programs in reading, spelling, listening, studying, etc., may be directed from here.

Probably co-operates with teaching departments in the training of counselors and other specialists in testing and counseling. May contribute to research in these fields.

TRANSCRIPT

Means TRANSCRIPT OF RECORD, the recorded results of your work in the classroom, with all important facts pertaining to your admission, classification and scholarship. Generally on file in the REGISTRAR'S OFFICE.

UNIVERSITY—COLLEGE—SCHOOL— DEPARTMENT

These designations are sometimes confusing. A UNIVERSITY is distinguished from an educational institution termed a COLLEGE by the fact that a UNIVERSITY provides professional training and generally a more extensive graduate program. A COLLEGE, on the other hand, is traditionally confined to a liberal arts curriculum.

The COLLEGE within a UNIVERSITY is generally a DIVISION OF THE UNIVERSITY which registers its own students, beginning with the freshman year. However, the distinction a COLLEGE and a SCHOOL WITHIN A UNIVERSITY is actually a matter of designation by faculty legislation. A SCHOOL is generally thought of as a division that admits students who have had certain preparatory or preliminary education required for entrance to the School. (Examples: Graduate School, for which a bachelor's degree is prerequisite; School of Law, requiring several years of pre-law study; School of Medicine, which specifies a certain amount of pre-medical study.)

DEPARTMENTS are simply divisions of either Schools or Colleges within Universities. DEPARTMENTS are usually headed by CHAIRMEN . . . SCHOOLS by DEANS OR DIRECTORS. Departments represent basic branches of learning on many campuses, but no absolute rule applies for determining what shall constitute a Department or how far its curriculum shall extend.

WORK LOAD (ACADEMIC)

The amount of credit work per week for which you, as a student, are registered. Usually designated in number of semester hours being taken for credit. Noncredit courses are sometimes given a semester-hour count in determining work loads which can be carried along with part-time employment. (*See* QUANTITY OF WORK RULE.)

ALLEN LUDDEN

has what he considers one of the most rewarding positions in television. As moderator of the award-winning television program "G.E. College Bowl," on the CBS Television Network, he serves as judge, referee, guide and—best of all—friend for the young adults competing in the weekly intercollegiate question-and-answer game. He asserts, "It's a pleasure to meet the youngsters from our colleges and universities and to watch how eagerly and expertly they handle the tough questions tossed at them."

An authority on youthful matters, Allen Ludden has written four helpful and stimulating books for teen- and college-agers. They are: *Plain Talk About College, Plain Talk for Men Under 21, Plain Talk for Women Under 21* and *Roger Thomas, Actor,* the latter a *Dodd, Mead Career Book.* In addition, he has written many articles for national magazines on the subject of young people and education.

Allen Ludden was born in Mineral Point, Wisconsin, and educated in Texas, receiving his master's degree in English from the University of Texas. While at the university, he found time to act in, publicize and direct productions of the dramatic society. His vacations were spent in Theatre Guild-sponsored summer stock companies in Westport, Connecticut, and Princeton, New Jersey. When he received his M.A. degree, he stayed on at his school as an English instructor, at the same time serving as director of the Austin (Texas) Little Theatre.

After working briefly at radio station KEYS, Corpus Christi, Allen Ludden entered the United States Army. While attached to an entertainment section in the Pacific, he served as executive production officer for Major Maurice Evans. He subsequently produced and directed more than forty Army shows. Upon his separation in 1946, with the rank of captain and after earning a Bronze Star, he rejoined Evans as personal manager. He remained with the Shakespearean actor until the spring of 1947, touring the country in advance of *Hamlet*. He next served as press agent for the summer theatre at Ivoryton, Connecticut, and soon after returned to radio, interviewing the stars from Ivoryton productions in a weekly "backstage" series on WTIC, Hartford.

Shortly thereafter he put together "Mind Your Manners," an NBC radio-television program that won national honors, including the Peabody and two Ohio State awards, and subsequently presided over the radio forerunner to the "G.E. College Bowl." He was also the star of "Dancetime," on television; was associated with "Young America," a segment of "Weekend"; and was moderator of "Teen-Age Forum" and the "Family Forum," on radio.

Currently, in addition to his Sunday role on the "G.E. College Bowl," he is serving full time as Director of Program Services for the CBS-owned Radio Stations.

Allen Ludden and his wife, Margaret, live in Dobbs Ferry, New York, with their three children, David, Martha and Sarah.